THE COMPATIBILITY OF COMPULSORY PURCHASE ORDERS AND HUMAN RIGHTS

By SHEMI LEIRA ESQ

For Sofia and Jeb

Disclaimer: Extensive steps have been taken to reference this work to other sources as appropriate.

Any reference or reproduction or quotes are not intended to infer ownership.

1st edition MAY 2019

Contents

Introduction

This text examines the compatibility of CPOs[1] and human rights.

Through the prism of the European Convention on human Rights which incorporates the Human rights Act 1998 and applicable international human rights conventions.

The text will focus on the compatibility of CPOs with the human rights of residents, tenants, homeowners or other parties with proprietary interests in the land with suggested proposals for reform. And analyse, the nexus and impact on residents' human rights.

Such as examining, inter alia, the right to a peaceful quiet enjoyment of one's home, *respect for the home (Art 8), fairness, transparency and the expeditious nature of the whole process (Art 6), equality of treatment (Art 14), freedom of association, expression (Art 9 and 10), Art 13 dealing with Just compensation or the appropriate legal remedies, Art 2(right to life), Equal treatment, impact on children and applicable international law.*

By analysing the underlying practical policies, practices and decisions. Such as consultation, internal processes, viability reports, environmental or equality matters, planning permission juxtaposed with the adverse impact on residents and settled communities.

Especially in fundamental life indicator areas, like employment, finances, culture, health and the disproportionate impact on racial minorities.[2] This also entails an imperative assessment of the applicable statutory compensation as to whether it is fair, just and equitable.[3] As well as challenge the compensation for CPOs affected residents for the cumulative injurious effects in many areas of people's lives. With particular focus on acquisitions by Local Authorities or public bodies which inevitably attaches the jurisdiction of ECHR and HRA. Juxtaposed with consideration as to whether the associated legal remedies are practically or meaningfully enforceable. Concluding with proposals for reform.

---

[1] Compulsory purchase orders , https://www.legislation.gov.uk/ukpga/1981/67/section/1

[2] 'It's not for us': Regeneration, the 2012 Olympics and the gentrification of East London, City, 2013

[3] Alice Belotti, Estate Regeneration and Community Impacts https://www.unicef.org/child-rights-conventionChallenges and lessons for social landlords, developers and local councils,2016

Chapter 1

Compulsory purchase orders[4], referred to as 'eminent domain'[5], in the United States, are a legal mechanism deployed by acquiring authorities to compulsorily acquire land[6] which may be occupied or encumbered with competing property or legal interests.[7]

CPOs 'require approval of a confirming minister under the Acquisition of Land Act 198'.[8] There are various 'enabling powers' available and the determination to authorise will partly depend on specific powers used.

Such public bodies with statutory powers include 'local authority's national park authorities, some executive agencies, the Homes and Communities Agency, health service bodies and government ministers'[9].

The Magna Carta,[10] under a historical royal prerogative by the crown[11], could also be used to acquire land.[12]

CPOs can further be implemented through acquisition of the freehold which should be distinguished from 'requisition', which is a form of 'possession' with interests, 'carved out of the estate'.[13]

The acquiring authority does not have to use a CPO to achieve its objectives and can acquire the freehold or let the leasehold expire.[14] Leading to an observation that a CPO is a 'euphemism' for imposed compensation on the landowner, without taking into account the gain by the acquiring party.[15]

CPO advocates point to benefits[16] such as 'social or affordable homes'[17] while critics argue that CPO schemes, undermine the financial, social, cultural and

---

[4] Compulsory purchase orders , https://www.legislation.gov.uk/ukpga/1981/67/section/1

[5] Jones, Stephen J. "Trumping eminent domain law: an argument for strict scrutiny analysis under the public use requirement of the Fifth Amendment." *Syracuse L. Rev.* 50 (2000): 285.

[6] /Knock It Down Or Do It Up pdf, https://www.london.gov.uk

[7] https://www.legislation.gov.uk/ukpga/1981/67/section/1

[8] f-guidance-on-compulsory-purchase-and-the-crichel-down-rules-for-the-disposal-of-surplus-land-.

[9] f-guidance-on-compulsory-purchase-and-the-crichel-down-rules-for-the-disposal-of-surplus-land-.

[10] chapter 29, pg. 8 evolution in the 18th and 19th century pg. 9; https://www.parliament.uk/magnacarta

[11] https://researchbriefings.parliament.uk/ResearchBriefing/Summary/SN03861

[12] Guy Roots, Michael Humphries, James Pereira, Robert Fookes The Law of Compulsory Purchase, pg. 13, 2011, 2nd Edition; Stephen Gadd,the-origin-of-statutory-compulsory-purchase-of-land-for-transport-development, https://archives.blog.parliament.uk, 22 September 2018

[13] Guy Roots, Michael Humphries, James Pereira, Robert Fookes The Law of Compulsory Purchase, pg. 13, 2011, 2nd Edition

[14] DCLG, Compulsory Purchase and Compensation to Residential Owners and Occupiers

[15] By Guy Roots, Michael Humphries, James Pereira, Robert Fookes The Law of Compulsory Purchase,

[16] Lord Adonis and Bill Davies, City villages: More homes, better communities, 2015

racial[18] fabric of longstanding communities,[19] leading to a detrimental impact in their lives[20].

DCLG guidance qualifies CPOs with a phrase, '*if used properly*', pointing to potential dis-benefits, reflected in the London Mayor's guidance[21] for estate regeneration and other reports.[22]

It is a key theme of this text, that CPOs are not inherently beneficial to communities, interfere with human rights[23] and are detrimental to longstanding settled residents, especially in the 'regeneration' of social housing or council estates.[24]

As the Aylesbury estate case ruling[25]indicated, there are consequential human rights detriments on settled communities. The *CPO in this case* was found to be inconsistent with the overall compelling test of the public interest, in breach of human rights of resident leaseholders[26] leading to observers to opine that the ruling could create a potentially 'new *right to community*'.[27]

The Secretary of state's conclusions, in Aylesbury, reflected concerns[28] that this amounted to displacing,[29] dislocating, disenfranchising, dispossessing communities, [30]worsening structural racial and social inequality in communities.[31]

As noted by Hubbard P and Lees, 'displacement is central to the process of gentrification... being removed from a place called home, the removal of the right to a property'.[32]
Other observers like Brett Christophers, refer to a wider context of a gradual process of privatisation of public land and public spaces.

---

[17]DownOrDoItUp_0.pdf,https://www.london.gov.uk/KnockIt down

[18]The-London-clearances-race-housing-and-policing http://www.irr.org.uk

[19]Demolition-watch-submission,http://www.demolitionwatchlondon.com, 14-march-2017,

[20] Alice Belotti, Challenges and lessons for social landlords, developers and local councils, 2016

[21] Better-homes-for-local-people-the-mayors-good-practice-guide-to-estate-regeneration.pdf, https://www.london.gov.uk/sites/default/files

[22] Knock it down or Do it up? The challenge of estate regeneration, February 2015

[23] Adélaïde Remiche, *Yordanova and Others v Bulgaria*: The Influence of the Social Right to Adequate Housing on the Interpretation of the Civil Right to Respect for One's Home, *Human Rights Law Review*, Volume 12, Issue 4, December 2012, Pages 787–800, https://doi.org/10.1093/hrlr/ngs033

[24] Hubbard P and Lees L, "The Right to Community?" (2018) 22 City 8

[25] Journal of Planning and Environment Law 17 Nov 2017 Compulsory purchase: life after Aylesbury

[26] Journal of Planning and Environment Law 17 Nov 2017 Compulsory purchase: life after Aylesbury

[27] Hubbard P and Lees L, "The Right to Community?" (2018) 22 City 8

[28] Social exclusion, Paul Watt (2013) 'It's not for us', City; Paul Watt, Housing Stock Transfers, Regeneration and State-Led Gentrification in London Article in Urban Policy and Research.

[29] Anne Rendell (2017) 'Arry's Bar: condensing and displacing on the Aylesbury Estate, The Journal of Architecture, 22:3, 532-554, DOI: 10.1080/13602365.2017.1310125

[30] Dispossession, The great social housing swindle, https://www.dispossessionfilm.com

[31] Alice Belotti, Challenges and lessons for social landlords, developers and local councils, 2016

[32] Hubbard P and Lees L, "The Right to Community?" (2018) 22 City 8

Arguing that there has been privatisation of public land over the long-term, in which CPOs are just part of the weapons in the tool box. Creating inequality and exclusion by private entities, monopolising access, or creating exclusive conditions for access and acceptance.[33]

A view echoed, by Anna Minton, when she questions whether the transformation of 'Britain's streets by the construction of new property, by private corporations, designed for profit, watched over by CCTV', has 'led to regeneration, which has made us more fearful of each other and intensified social divisions'.[34]

This is further described as a 'class tool' to undermine working class communities, through 'stigmatisation or demonization' of mainly 'poor urban neighbourhoods' and a 'fictionalised mantra of necessity' combined with 'neo liberal logics with an 'obscene underside'[35].

But perhaps most suitably legally contextually simplified by Justice Scalia in KELO[36], when he stated that, *'what this lady wants is not more money. No amount of money is going to satisfy her. She is living in this house... her whole life and she does not want to move.*

She said I'll move if it's being taken for a public use, but by God, you're just giving it to some other private individual because that individual is going to pay more taxes. I -- it seems to me that's, that's an objection in principle, and an objection in principle that the public use requirement of the Constitution seems to be addressed to '.

CPOs therefore appear to be just part of the tools utilised in 'neoliberal Britain'[37] to legally acquire land that may inherently create inequality, social divisions and leading to human right breaches. Which is consistent with the secretary's observation in the Aylesbury case and other indications that CPOs are major tools of the gentrification process displacing long standing settled communities.[38]

Hence the need for CPOs to be viewed as 'exceptional measures' that warrant scrutiny through 'political struggle' and 'policy practice'.[39]

---

[33] Brett Christophers, The New Enclosures, the Appropriation of Public Land in Neoliberal Brit

[34] Anna Minton, Ground Control, Fear and Happiness in the twenty first century City

[35] Gray, N., and Porter, L. (2015), By Any Means Necessary: Urban Regeneration and the "State of Exception" in Glasgow's Commonwealth Games 2014, *Antipode*, 47, 380– 400, doi: 10.1002/anti.12114

[36] Kelo *v. CITY OF NEW LONDON (125 S.Ct. 2655 (2005)[1],*

[37] Brett Christophers, The New Enclosures, the Appropriation of Public Land in Neoliberal Brit

[38] Alice Belotti, Challenges and lessons for social landlords, developers and local councils, 2016

[39] Neil Gray Libby Porter, By Any Means Necessary: Urban Regeneration and the "State of Exception" in Glasgow's Commonwealth

Since challenging CPOs in courts through measures such as judicial reviews, despite some successes[40] does not ensure halting CPOs, per se.[41]

Residents, usually litigants in person or with no legal training, compete against local authorities with substantial financial resources. Especially, due to the imbalance of resources, power or where there is potential imminent risk to human health, it would be assumed that the balance of priorities should be weighted in favour of protecting the vulnerable, less powerful is socio-economic terms and risks to health[42].

This raises questions about the effectiveness of judicial review or 'a general right of judicial review', in addressing complex issues, such as 'decisions to vest land that is the 'subject of a confirmed compulsory order.'[43]
Thus creating an urgent need for analysis of the compatibility of CPOs with human rights.[44]

But it is important to first highlight the adverse impact on residents[45] due to CPO based acquisitions such as estate 'regeneration'.[46]

Chapter 2

Overview of impact of CPOs

Compulsory acquisition schemes especially in social housing are promoted[47] as beneficial to residents, despite the documented economic, social and environmental dis-benefits. Leading to adverse impact on health, family life, finance,[48] social and racial equality, [49]manifested by the disproportionate, detrimental effect on racial minorities who are over represented in social housing.[50]

Games 2014

[40] BOKROSOVA v LONDON BOROUGH OF LAMBETH[2015] EWHC 3386 (Admin)

[41] R-Plant-v-Lambeth-London-Borough-Council-2016-EWHC-3324-Admin.doc

[42] Hodkinson, S., & Essen, C. (2015). Grounding accumulation by dispossession in everyday life. International Journal of Law in the Built Environment, 7(1), 72-91.

[43] Jonathan Ferris, Journal of Planning & Environmental review, 2010

[44]Towards_a_Compulsory_Purchase_Code1_Summary.pdf

[45] *the-real-cost-of-regeneration-social-housing-private-developers-pfi, https://www.theguardian.com/society/2017/jul/21/*

[46]demolition-watch-submission-14-march-2017.pdf http://www.demolitionwatchlondon.com

[47] Lord Adonis and Bill Davies, City villages: More homes, better communities, 2015

[48] Alice Belotti, Estate Regeneration and Community Impacts Challenges and lessons for social landlords, developers and local councils,2016

[49] London Inequality, https://www.runnymedetrust.org; https://www.gov.uk/government/publications/race-disparity-audit

[50] The-London-clearances-race-housing-and-policing, http://www.irr.org.uk

The Runnymede Trust reported disproportionate social and racial inequality, [51]leading to intergenerational consequences caused by the "dislocation from family life", community, potential harm to the education of affected children and employment opportunities.[52]

Leaseholders face dissolution of their mortgages, undervalued homes, higher unaffordable valuations of the new homes[53] or offered shared ownerships which are detrimental to their property rights and financial interests.

Obligating them to use their savings, equity or compensation, to get a share of the new property, destroying any financial security for families.[54] Residents are subjected to protracted processes of negotiations for compensation, accommodation, rehousing[55] and disruption.[56]

Worse, compensation does not always enable residents to buy on the open market in the same locality leading to displacement, despite statutory provisions, [57]central government guidance[58]and regional policies[59]. Compensation is not within a free market competition, per se, in its ordinary sense. Since properties are under a demolition notice, sold in very specific timelines, to a sole buyer, possibly also the acquiring party, leading to high housing costs for those compelled to stay.[60]

Consigning them to a life, future of financial or property servitude, exploitation and subservience to the freeholder. While rights of succession are curtailed or extinguished for tenants. Creating dispossession of outright ownership or life tenure to complete subservience, disenfranchisement, and hindrance of social mobility.[61]

In some cases, councils[62] undermine collective democratically and constitutionally elected independent residents organisations or representatives[63],

---

[51] London Inequality, https://www.runnymedetrust.org

[52] Watt, Paul. "It's Not for Us: Regeneration, the 2012 Olympics and the Gentrification of East London." City 17, no. 1 (2013): 99-11

[53] Lucy Thomas, JOURNAL OF PLANNING AND ENVIRONMENT LAW 17 NOV 2017 Compulsory purchase: life after Aylesbury

[54] Lucy Thomas, JOURNAL OF PLANNING AND ENVIRONMENT LAW 17 NOV 2017 Compulsory purchase: life after Aylesbury

[55] https://architectsforsocialhousing.wordpress.com/2018/09/07; the-costs-of-estate-regeneration: Watt, Paul. "It's Not for Us: Regeneration, the 2012 Olympics and the Gentrification of East London." City 17, no. 1 (2013): 99-11.

[56] /better-homes-for-local-people-the-mayors-good-practice-guide-to-estate-regeneration.pdf
https://www.london.gov.uk

[57] S39 Land compensation act 1973,

[58] DCLG Guidance on compulsory purchase orders

[59] Better homes for local people THE MAYOR'S GOOD PR ACTICE GUIDE TO ESTATE REGENER ATION FEBRUARY 2018

[60] The-story-of-the-Camberwell-submarine, https://www.insidehousing.co.uk/insight/insight

[61] Alice Belotti, Estate Regeneration and Community Impacts Challenges and lessons for social landlords, developers and local councils,2016

marginalising residents,[64] not to mention the rise in anti-Social behaviour and disrepair.[65]

In cases, such as the Heygate estate[66], with around 198 homes, the process took around 10 years until November 2013. It's estimated that around 45 tenants had returned to live in the new homes out of the 0riginal 1000 secure tenants.[67]

Some leaseholders[68] who are unable to transfer their existing mortgage for any reason, are not always awarded compensation that equitably reflects the associated spiral human effects of being displaced from a settled community including especially young children.[69]

Residents face an obscure process hindering their property rights[70]displacing leaseholders into costly private accommodation in the locality,[71]use of 'escrow'[72] or a cap on specific amount of their savings in relation to rehousing or compensation.[73]

Statutory requests for advance payments to cater for associated costs are unreasonably delayed or even denied to alleviate the financial burden of those forced to move into private accommodation or costs associated with CPOs home loss, diminishing any savings, capital and compensation.[74]

Resident home owners may be subject to means assessment[75] leading to questionable management practices[76] or aim of regeneration.[77]

Residents have raised governing concerns, conflict of interests related to occupancy, ownership, possession or peaceful enjoyment of their homes[78]. The

---

[62] staying-put-web-version-low, https://justspacelondon.files.wordpress.com/2014/06/
[63]

[64] housing-scandal-one-council-to-choose-who-represents-tenants-and-leaseholders-on-new-residents-assembly/, https://newsfromcrystalpalace.wordpress.com/2017/11/08

[65] Dispossession, the great housing swindle, https://www.dispossessionfilm.com/

[66] Loretta Lees, Mara Ferreri, Resisting gentrification on its final frontiers: Learning from the Heygate Estate in London (1974–2013),Cities, Volume 57,2016,Pages 14-24,https://doi.org/10.1016/j.cities.2015.12.005, http://www.sciencedirect.com

[67] Lucy Thomas, JOURNAL OF PLANNING AND ENVIRONMENT LAW 17 NOV 2017 Compulsory purchase: life after Aylesbury

[68] Lucy Thomas, JOURNAL OF PLANNING AND ENVIRONMENT LAW 17 NOV 2017 Compulsory purchase: life after Aylesbury

[69]Heygate-estate/heygate-displacement-maps, https://southwarknotes.wordpress.com

[70] Staying Put, An Anti-gentrification Handbook, for council estates in London

[71] Aylesbury-cpo_decision-letter_final.pdf, https://southwarknotes.files.wordpress.com/2009/12

[72] Lucy Thomas, JOURNAL OF PLANNING AND ENVIRONMENT LAW 17 NOV 2017 Compulsory purchase: life after Aylesbury

[73] Aylesbury-cpo_decision-letter_final.pdf, https://southwarknotes.files.wordpress.com/2009/12

[74] https://www.theguardian.com/society/2017/jul/21/the-real-cost-of-regeneration-social-housing-private-developers-pfi

[75] Draft-good-practice-guide-to-estate-regeneration-main-consultation-summary-report.pdf https://www.london.gov.uk

[76] Beswick, J. and Penny, J. (2018), Demolishing the Present to Sell off the Future? The Emergence of 'Financialized Municipal Entrepreneurialism' in London. Int. J. Urban Reg. Res., 42: 612-632. doi:10.1111/1468-2427.12612

[77] Stuart Hodkinson, Chris Essen, (2015) "Grounding accumulation by dispossession in everyday life: The unjust geographies of urban regeneration under the Private Finance Initiative", International Journal of Law in the Built Environment, Vol. 7 Issue: 1, pp.72-91, https://doi.org/10.1108/IJLBE-01-2014-0007

legal implication of the development schemes raises questions about safeguards for residents' legal and property rights.[79]

In some boroughs[80], new leases or tenancy agreements appear intrusive or restrictive. Especially for residents who had full ownership prior to the 'regeneration' save being subject to a mortgage while compensation does not fully address the associated spiral human effects of being displaced from a settled community especially with young children.[81].

There is a lack of transparency from developers, surveyors, architects, or local authorities. Especially in cases of viability reports, described as the 'dark art of viability' aimed at secrecy and avoidance of mitigation measures associated with adverse impacts of the developments, to maximise the propensity to 'inflate profits.[82]

Sometimes, the successful progress of CPOs is contractually attached to s106[83] agreements or confidential agreements between councils and private developers. Funded by public money, building on public land, causing adverse impact on settled communities without any apparent or minimal 'public good' or 'council homes'.[84]

Cumulatively, the process[85] from the initial decision, consultation, compensation, construction is one littered with a lack of transparency, imbalance of power, dispossession, distress[86] and dislocation of settled communities.[87]

That is a synopsis of the associated adverse impact of CPOs in cases such as estate regeneration, which requires a detailed examination of compatibility with

---

[78] https://www.whatdotheyknow.com/request/special_purpose_vehicles_formed

[79] Hubbard P and Lees L, "The Right to Community?" (2018) 22 City 8

[80] http://estateregeneration.lambeth.gov.uk/key_guarantees

[81] Jane Rendell (2017) 'Arry's Bar: condensing and displacing on the Aylesbury Estate, The Journal of Architecture, 22:3, 532-554, DOI: 10.1080/13602365.2017.1310125

[82] Rebecca Warren, A review of the trend towards greater transparency and public access to information in the planning arena with a particular focus on viability appraisals, Journal of Planning and Environmental law, 2015

[83] https://www.local.gov.uk/pas/pas-topics/infrastructure/s106-obligations-overview

[84] http://35percent.org/heygate-regeneration-faq/

[85] westbury_estate_minutes_from_public ,https://issuu.com/catherinemakegood/docs/

[86] mental-health-issues-being-ignored-on-estates-lambeth-council-want-to-demolish-and-so-are-human-rights-issues-cabinet-told-its-a-game-to you,
https://newsfromcrystalpalace.wordpress.com/2017/03/24/ you/

[87] By Dr Sarah Bel, Social and health Impact of regeneration The review concluded that in general refurbishment of social housing is technically feasible and environmentally preferable to demolition; Estate Regeneration and Community Impacts Challenges and lessons for social Landlords, developers and local councils, Case report 99,Alice Belotti LSE Housing & Communities March 2016

Human rights a central focus here. Through analysis of the justification, process, compensation, and possible remedies.

Chapter 3

CPO Jurisdiction, powers, exercise and justification

Parliament legislated for the 'taking of property' in the interests of the 'public good' followed by a specified process. This can be characterised as the legal 'taking of property' in the interests of the 'public good' and requires a specified legislated process[88] under compulsory purchase procedures.[89]

DCLG requirements, state that, *'most acts containing enabling powers specify that the procedures in the Acquisition of Land Act 1981, apply to orders made under those powers and an acquiring authority must follow those procedures'.*[90]

The acquiring party files an application to a minister of state, stating the purpose of the CPO, a specific property, justification and compensation.[91]

If satisfied, the government inspector makes a recommendation to the Secretary of state[92]. However objectors can challenge the CPO as specified in the guidance.[93]

Source of CPO Powers

CPOs are commonly invoked under a specific act of parliament or Transport and Works act 1992[94]. The invoked act depends on the specific body or reason for the CPOs.

These include, inter alia, *the Land clauses consolidation act 1845, Railway clauses consolidation act 1845, the general use Local government Act 1933, the Planning Act 2008 for a Nationally Significant Infrastructure Project, Crossrail Act 2008, in relation to specified land rather than the UK as a whole, the Harbours Act 1964, s.226 of the Town and country planning Act 1990, Part 2 of town and planning act 1997, Neighbourhood Planning Act 2017 which grants powers to the Mayor of London for regeneration and housing tLGA1972,*

---

[88] guidance-on-compulsory-purchase-and-the-crichel-down-rules-for-the-disposal-of-surplus-land-.pdf

[89] https://www.legislation.gov.uk/1981/67/section/2

[90] DCLG guidance on compulsory purchase orders

[91] -guidance-on-compulsory-purchase-and-the-crichel-down-rules-for-the-disposal-of-surplus-land

[92] Secretary of state

[93] DCLG

[94] https://www.gov.uk/government/publications/compulsory-purchase-and-compensation-booklet-1-procedure

S142 of LGPA1980, S17 of HA1985 , s47 PA1990, ss29.s34 and 300 HA1985,s93(2) LGHA1989, s59 of the Airport Act 1986 and powers for wider purposes like 'education' under s530 of EA1996 and S203-206 of the HPA2016, which legislates for 'third party' rights to be extinguished for developmental land or 'planning purposes.

CPOs can also be triggered by 'an owner serving purchase notices; or a blight notice under section 150 of the section 150 of the Town and Country Planning 1990 Act, only served in the circumstances listed in schedule 13 to that act 8'.[95]

There is a historical royal prerogative by the crown to acquire land in war time. Hence [96] CPOs being described as a 'euphemism' for imposed compensation, as indicated above.[97] Its contemporary application is questionable save in 'exceptional circumstances'.[98] Government guidance, *emphasises that , 'public bodies with statutory powers, such as 'local authorities statutory undertakers, some executive agencies, the Homes and Communities Agency, health service bodies, Government ministers, will have their own internal guidance on how to proceed'.[99]*

CPO powers related to housing and 'estate regeneration'

Local authorities,[100]can use 'section 226 of the Town and Country Planning Act 1990', county, district or London borough councils[101],joint planning boards[102] and national park authorities [103] to acquire land compulsorily for development, for 'housing' purposes[104].

As well as the Housing Act 1985: Part 2, [105]S17 of the Housing Act 1985',[106] s29, s300 of the Housing Act 1985, s34 of the Housing Associations Act 1985, Local Government Housing Act 1989 under Part 7 of the Local Government and Housing Act 1989 and s93(2) of the Local Government and Housing Act 1989'[107].

---

[95] guidance-on-compulsory-purchase-and-the-crichel-down-rules-for-the-disposal-of-surplus-land-pdf

[96] Guy Roots, Michael Humphries, James Pereira, Robert Fookes The Law of Compulsory Purchase, pg. 13 By Guy Roots, Michael Humphries, James Pereira, Robert Fookes The Law of Compulsory Purchase.

[97] Guy Roots, Michael Humphries, James Pereira, Robert Fookes The Law of Compulsory Purchase, pg. 13 By Guy Roots, Michael Humphries, James Pereira, Robert Fookes The Law of Compulsory Purchase.

[98] *Barry Denyer-Green,* Compulsory Purchase and Compensation,Edition10th Edition,2013

[99] https://www.gov.uk/government/publications/compulsory-purchase-and-compensation-booklet-1-procedure

[100] https://moderngov.lambeth.gov.uk/documents/CPOCabinetReport Westbury.pdf

[101] section 2268

[102] (section 2441

[103] (section 244A)

[104] Section 246(1).

[105] *which relates to the Provision of housing accommodation under S17 of the Housing Act 1985*

[106] https://www.gov.uk/government/publications/compulsory-purchase-process-and-the-crichel-down-rules-guidance

[107] https://www.gov.uk/government/publications/compulsory-purchase-process-and-the-crichel-down-rules-guidance

Restrictions are placed *under section 226(1A), that the 'acquiring authority must not exercise the power unless they think that the proposed development, redevelopment or improvement is likely to contribute to achieving the promotion or improvement of the economic, social or environmental well- being of the area for which the acquiring authority has administrative responsibility.'*[108] Government guidance further stipulates that, *'orders will be considered on their merits…. that there should be a compelling case for compulsory purchase in the public interest.'*[109]

Statutory compensation

Part of the process requires statutory compensation under the Land compensation Act 1961, Compulsory Purchase Act 1965, LCA 1965 and LCA1973[110], acquisition of the Land Act 1981 and CPQ (Vesting Declarations) 1981.[111]

There are amendments by the Localism Act 2011[112] of Land compensation Act 1961 to rehousing, compensation payment of disturbance fees and home loss payments, in various statues[113] and DCLG guidance.[114]

Central government guidance further states tha*t, 'where acquiring authorities arrange to acquire land by agreement, they will pay compensation as if it had not been compulsorily purchased.*[115]The principle was laid down by Lock Blackburn[116] to put the claimant in money terms, in the same position they would have been in but for the CPO.[117]

The prime issue[118] is whether the statutory compensation is equitable, just and fair. The loss suffered is more than just a physical structure. The impact is attaches to the home, home environment, community, cultural attachments,

---

[108] DCLG guidelines, https://www.gov.uk/government/publications/compulsory-purchase-process-and-the-crichel-down-rules-guidance

[109] https://www.gov.uk/government/publications/compulsory-purchase-process-and-the-crichel-down-rules-guidance

[110] Land compensation acts

[111] Michael Barnes, The Law of compulsory purchase and compensation

[112] Denyer-Green, B. (2014). Compulsory Purchase and Compensation. London: Estates Gazette.

[113] Such as LCA 1973, Localism Act 2011, inter alia

[114] Compulsory_purchase_process_and_the_Crichel_Down_Rules_-_guidance_updated
,https://assets.publishing.service.gov.uk

[115] DCLG guidance cited above

[116] Livingstone V Rayward Railway company(1880)

[117] Denyer-Green, B. (2014). Compulsory Purchase and Compensation. London: Estates Gazette.

[118] See A1P1 and compensation below

support networks, education, employment, faith centres[119] and incremental inequality.[120]

It should be emphasised that this is not an exhaustive description of sources of CPO powers and it's not the purpose of this dissertation to examine these powers, per se, but to assess the overall compatibility of the use CPO powers with the human rights of those in 'situ' or with property interests.

Attempts by the law commission to issue a new statutory code for compensation and process have been futile despite the publication of two reports in 2003 and 2004 respectively.[121]

Inevitably CPO's are challenged for the lack of proven 'compelling public interest' and inadequate compensation, described as a cover for 'social cleansing'.[122]

As highlighted above, for residents, the process and outcome is not always fair, just and equitable. Leading to loss of property rights, emotional distress and related detriments due to compelled displacement especially long standing communities. They argue that he fundamental need for 'a place' or community', a right to community and that 'compensation' should be beyond 'financial compensation' per se' for the loss of property, but adequate compensation for losing a home. This is suggestive of an expanded notion of housing rights that encompasses 'a right to community' something that raises the possibility of the law actually aligning with the interests of council residents rather than supporting the politics of gentrification[123].

The London Mayor states that 'Social housing has been central to making London the greatest city in the world, but when done badly, we know estate regeneration can result in disagreement, which can leave residents feeling they have not been properly consulted, social housing being lost, and displaced tenants and leaseholders getting a bad deal'. Although the London Mayor's critics argue that he has failed to use his powers of funding and housing over London to protect existing long standing settled communities from the detrimental impact of estate 'regeneration'.[124]

---

[119] https://www.gov.uk/government/publications/compulsory-purchase-and-compensation-booklet-1-procedure

[120] https://www.runnymedetrust.org/projects-and-publications/equality-and-integration/london-ethnic-inequalities.html

[121] Law Com no 286,(2003) and No 281(20014)

[122] https://www.architectsjournal.co.uk, Estate-regeneration-why-people-power-is-forcing-london-to-rethink-housing/1002832https://architectsforsocialhousing.wordpress.com/2016/03/24/the-doomsday-book; Phil Hubbard, Loretta Lees. (2018) The right to community?. City 22:1, pages 8-25.; https://www.transparency.org.uk/faulty-towers; Paul Watt (2009) Housing Stock Transfers, Regeneration and State-Led Gentrification in London, Urban Policy and Research, 27:3, 229-242, DOI: 10.1080/08111140903154147 5.article

[124] Mayor of London. 2014. Homes for London: The London Housing strategy. London: GLA.

THE COMPATIBILITY OF COMPULSORY PURCHASE ORDERS AND HUMAN RIGHTS © 2019 SHEMI LEIRA ESQUIRE

A similar sentiment cited by the report, 'Faulty Towers' which states that, "While Londoners find themselves priced out of the capital, many new homes are left unused by wealthy investors based overseas demand for London property is fuelled by the corruption that robs public services of vital funds all around the world. Others feel the need to move their legitimate wealth here out of fear of what might happen to it in countries where corruption is endemic or has brought instability in times of crisis."

Therefore, 'claims' that local residents are the beneficiaries, of CPO effected social housing regeneration, in addition to the inadequacy of compensation and its restriction in monetary terms, are strongly disputed by residents, supporters, architects , campaigners , NGOs and academics.

The report,[125]'Faulty Towers',[126] highlights a significant issue, stating that, *"while Londoners find themselves priced out of the capital, many new homes are left unused by wealthy investors based overseas' and 'demand for London property is fuelled by the corruption that robs public services of vital funds all around the world'.*[127]

Echoing similar complaints by architects, [128]experts, [129]NGOs[130] and academics.[131] Crystalized by Justice Scalia in KELO *v. CITY OF NEW LONDON (125 S.Ct. 2655 (2005)[132]*, when he states that, *'what this lady wants is not more money. No amount of money is going to satisfy her. She is living in this house... her whole life and she does not want to move. She said I'll move if it's being taken for a public use, but by God, you're just giving it to some other private individual because that individual is going to pay more taxes. That, it seems to me, just washes out entirely the distinction between private use and public use'.*[133]

---

https://www.architectsjournal.co.uk/news/estate-regeneration-why-people-power-is-forcing-london-to-rethink-housing/10028325.article; https://www.insidehousing.co.uk/news/news/mayor-and-conservatives-dispute-latest-london-housing-stats-57545

[125] Douglas Maxwell, Journal of planning & Environmental Law, Article 1 of the First protocol: A paper tiger in the face of compulsory purchase orders for private profit?

[126] faulty-towers-understanding-the-impact-of-overseas-corruption-on-the-london-property-market/ https://www.transparency.org.uk

[127] https://www.transparency.org.uk/press-releases/faulty-towers/

[128] https://architectsforsocialhousing.wordpress.com/2016/03/24/the-doomsday-book/)

[129] Phil Hubbard, Loretta Lees. (2018) The right to community? *City* 22:1, pages 8-25.

[130] https://www.transparency.org.uk/faulty-towers/

[131] Paul Watt (2009) Housing Stock Transfers, Regeneration and State-Led Gentrification in London, Urban Policy and Research, 27:3, 229-242, DOI: 10.1080/08111140903154147

[132] [1] https://www.supremecourt.gov/oral_arguments/argument_transcripts/2004/04-108.pdf

[133] [1] https://www.supremecourt.gov/oral_arguments/argument_transcripts/2004/04-108.pdf

A succinct criticism associated with CPOs which require justification prior to authorisation.

Chapter 4

Legal justification of CPOs

CPO processes require legal justification for interfering with one's home or property rights, a nexus between the exercise of CPO powers and a public benefit.[134]

There are broader principles such as the public interest, human rights, public sector Equality Duty, viability, funding and alternatives discussed in more detail below

For estate 'regeneration',[135] legal justification,[136] should demonstrate *inter alia, a 'compelling case in the public interest', compatibility with ECHR, consideration of a public sector equality duty[137], funding sources, viability tests, alternatives to CPO, planning considerations and negotiations with the landowners.* But this may vary from the specific CPO cited power and rationale.

Government guidance,[138] further states that, '*when making and confirming an order, acquiring authorities and authorising authorities should be sure that the purposes for which the compulsory purchase order is made justify interfering with the human rights of those with an interest in the land affected. The officers report seeking authorisation for the compulsory purchase order should address human rights issues...particular consideration should be given to the provisions of Article 1 of the First Protocol to the European Convention on Human Rights and, in the case of a dwelling, Article 8 of the Convention*'.

CPOs can therefore, inter alia be challenged for procedural flaws, [139]adherence to statutory provisions, compatibility with human rights, proportionality and public interest requirements discussed below.

---

[134] See Lord denning in Prest v SOS for wales 1982 who cited Forbes in Brown V SOS for the environment ;Mentions R v SOS transport exparte p de Rothschild, pg. 16; SAINSBURY'S SUPERMARKETS LTD, REGINA (ON THE APPLICATION OF) V WOLVERHAMPTON CITY COUNCIL AND ANOTHER: SC 12 MAY 2010; December 20, 2018 admin Off Planning, sainsbury_wolverhampton References: [2010] UKSC 20, [2010] RVR 237, [2010] 20 EG 144, [2010] PTSR 1103, [2010] 2 WLR 1173

[135] *section 226(1)(a) enables acquiring authorities with planning powers to acquire land if they think that it will facilitate the carrying out of development (as defined in section 55 of Town and Country Planning Act 1990)*

[136] See David Elvin QC, Use of compulsory purchase powers for regeneration, 2017

[137] S149 of EA2010

[138] guidance-on-compulsory-purchase-and-the-crichel-down-rules-for-the-disposal-of-surplus-land-pdf

[139] Bokrosova V Lambeth; http://www.bailii.org/ew/cases/EWHC/Admin/2015/3386.html

Public interest

Satisfying the public interest 'compelling case', criteria is one of the prerequisites for a CPO confirmation.[140] The court 'quashed[141]' a CPO stating that, while 'in principle' refusal of planning permission does not hinder authorisation of a CPO, the 'facts' of the case indicated that the CPO was confirmed on the basis of an application for the 'public benefit', without 'sufficiently compelling justification for the public interest'.[142]

Government guidance states that, 'a compulsory purchase order should only be made where there is a compelling case in the public interest. ..a balanced view between the intentions of the acquiring authority, the concerns of those with an interest in the land that it is proposing to acquire compulsorily and the wider public interest'.[143]

As Laws J states, [144] *'it is enough that ownership in land is recognised as a constitutional right, as Lord Denning said it was. Only another interest, a public interest, of greater interest, may override it', followed by a requirement to pay full and fair compensation'.*

If established, the interference has to be proportionate to the stated aim. A fair balance test is applied, examining a legitimate aim to justify restriction, rational connection to the aim, less intrusive means and the benefits are contrasted with dis-benefits, which exceeds the judicial review tests in UK courts.

Public Sector Equality Duty[145]

The guidance stipulates *that 'the purposes for which the compulsory purchase order is made', should 'justify interfering with the human rights of those with an interest in the land affected.[146]*

---

[140] In *Grafton Group (UK) v Sec of state*

[141] In *Grafton Group (UK) v Sec of State*

[142] Saira Kabir Sheikh QC, J.P .L, 2015

[143] https://assets.publishing.service.gov.uk/government/uploads/system/uploads/attachment_data/file/475271/cpo_guidance.pdf

[144] Chesterfield Properties Place v Sec of State(1997) 76 P & CR 117

[145] Public sector duty, under s149 of EA2010

[146] -guidance-on-compulsory-purchase-and-the-crichel-down-rules-for-the-disposal-of-surplus-land-pdf

Including a public sector duty requirement by public authorities in exercising compulsory purchase powers.[147] Holgate J determined as unlawful, a 'policy' where there was a 'failure to have proper regard to the public sector equality duty', in reference to 'affordable housing, social infrastructure contributions and a vacancy credit policy'.[148]

The Guidance further emphasises that, *"all public sector acquiring authorities are bound by the Public Sector Equality Duty as set out in section 149 of the Equality Act 2010. In exercising their compulsory purchase and related powers (e.g. powers of entry) these acquiring authorities must have regard to the effect of any differential impacts on groups with protected characteristics. For example, an important use of compulsory purchase powers is to help regenerate run down areas. Although low income is not a protected characteristic it is not uncommon for people from ethnic minorities, the elderly or people with a disability to be overrepresented in low income groups. As part of the Public Sector Equality Duty, acquiring authorities must have due regard to the need to promote equality of opportunity between persons who share a relevant protected characteristic and persons who do not share it.*

This might mean that the acquiring authority devises a process which promotes equality of opportunity by addressing particular problems that people with certain protected characteristics might have (e.g. making sure that documents are accessible for people with sight problems or learning difficulties and that people have access to advocates or advice.[149]

However, this is often inadequate, such as where a council lawyer expressed doubt or surprise as to how the PSED would apply to racial minorities.[150]The process and substance appear self-serving where the acquiring body drives the 'impact assessment'. Other considerations for confirming a CPO include funding, viability and other alternatives to CPOs[151].

Financial considerations

Financial matters appear to be regarded as matters for confirming authorities or financial experts to be taken into account,[152] requiring transparency to assess the public interest.

---

[147] In R (on the application of Reading BC v SoS DCL

[148] Saira Kabir Sheikh QC,JPL, 2015

[149] Cpo guidance, https://assets.publishing.service.gov.uk

[150] Lambeth council lawyer, apart from disability, his client did not understand how THI applied to racial minorities; https://twitter.com/saveWestburySW8; https://www.facebook.com/Savewestburysw8-804075296314550/; Human Rights today blog

[151] guidance-on-compulsory-purchase-and-the-crichel-down-rules-for-the-disposal-of-surplus-land

[152] R Plant V Lambeth London Borough Council [2016] EWHC 3324 (Admin)

DCLG guidance states that, *in preparing its justification, the acquiring authority should address: The 'sources and timing of that funding and only in exceptional circumstances would it be reasonable to acquire land with little prospect of the scheme being implemented for a number of years'*[153].

From the residents perspective,[154] there are questions regarding, interest, security, control, profit, public land as security, governance, divestment of interest[155], repayments or interest on the loan,[156] which require full and complete transparency of financial sources[157], contracts and s106 agreements.[158]

S106 Agreements

S106 agreements[159] provide alternative proposals to applications that would otherwise be unsuccessful.[160] Such as 'pre-commencement' conditions or restrictions during construction, regarding the use of the 'development' and mitigation factors[161] measured by key tests.[162]

There are competing arguments about the use or disclosure of s.106[163] which may impact viability of the projects.[164]The court in *Perry* held that viability reports are confidential due to sensitive 'commercial information regarding costs or residential values'. In contrast to *Turner V SOS*, the court held that, a local authority should disclose viability report if requested by the SOS.

The issues were whether developers applying for planning permission, had to submit a report regarding the level of 'affordable housing', to aid objectors to challenge the decision[165].Government guidance, indicates that the balance should be weighted towards public availability, at least as an 'executive summary', in exceptional circumstances while[166] campaigners[167], demand full disclosure.[168] .

---

153 Cpo_guidance https://assets.publishing.service.gov.uk

154 http://www.thepeoplesaudit.info/open-letter-to-andrew-travers-lambeth-council-chief-executive-august-2018/

155 Estate_Regeneration_National_Strategy Resident_Engagement_and_Protection, https://assets.publishing.service.gov.uk

156 See Homes For Lambeth business plan, minutes of cabinet, 4th March 2019, regarding concerns from residents et al, https://moderngov.lambeth.gov.uk: https://www.homesforlambeth.co.uk/

157 Estate_Regeneration_National_Strategy_-_Financing_and_Delivering_Estate_Regeneration https://assets.publishing.service.gov.uk

158 https://www.gov.uk/guidance/planning-obligations

159 http://www.legislation.gov.uk/ukpga/1990/8/section/106

160The_decision-making_process, https://www.planningportal.co.uk

161 https://www.gov.uk/guidance/planning-obligations

162 https://www.gov.uk/guidance/planning-obligations

163 R(on application of Perry) V Hackney LBC

164 Saira Kabir Sheikh QC, J.P .L, 2015

165 https://www.gov.uk/guidance/viability#accountability

166 https://www.gov.uk/guidance/viability#accountability

167 http://35percent.org/images/viabilityfordummies.pdf; communities-open-the-book-for-viability-assessments,

Raising a question as to why would entire settled communities be displaced or dislocated in the absence of verifiable proof of social housing or affordable housing or a beneficiary.

Alternatives to CPOs

Government guidance refers to examination of 'whether the purpose for which the acquiring authority is proposing to acquire land, could be achieved by any other means, for its reuse or any alternative location'.[169]

However, the possibility of an alternative does not negate the existence of a 'compelling case in the public interest'. As held in *James,* [170]'the availability of alternative solutions does not itself render the leasehold reform legislation unjustified'. It's one of the 'factors relevant for determining whether the means chosen could be regarded as reasonable and suited to achieving the legitimate aim pursued, having regard to the need to strike a 'fair balance.[171]

As David Elvin Qc observes,[172], the court appears not to have embraced stricter criteria in determining alternatives to 'proportionality', 'fair balance',[173]suitable locations for the purpose of acquisition'[174]and the right considerations by the Secretary of state'.[175]

If considered properly, alternatives to CPO schemes could cause impediments.[176]

Planning determinations

Government guidance [177] refers to a need for planning permission assessments to reflect a 'compelling case in the public interest', emphasising that *'justification for a scheme linked to proposals identified in the development plan, will be given due weight and the national planning policy is a material consideration in all planning decisions'.*

In *Grafton*, where prospective planning permission was the reason for grant of CPO confirmation, the Judge stressed that the compelling public interest test

---

[168] London Borough of Southwark v Lend lease 09.05.14, http://informationrights.decisions.tribunals.gov.uk

[169] guidance-on-compulsory-purchase-and-the-crichel-down-rules-for-the-disposal-of-surplus-land-pd

[170] James V UK(1986 8 E H R R 123 at (51)

[171] 'Mutatis mutandis, the Klass and Others judgement of September 1978.'

[172] Also discussed in David Elvin Qc, 2017, The use of compulsory purchase powers for regeneration

[173] R (Clays Lane Housing Cooperative ltd V Housing Corp(2005)1 WLR 2229

[174] Swish Estates Ltd and another v Secretary of State for Communities & Local Government and another [2017] EWHC 3331

[175] See Pascoe V First Secretary of State (2007), R (Hall) V first Secretary of State (2007) 1 W. L.R 885 Nand Bexley LBC V SOS(2001) where alternatives were issues at court.

[176] http://cressinghampeoplesplan.org.uk/; PeoplesPlanDevelopmentAppraisal.pdf https://moderngov.lambeth.gov.uk

[177] guidance-on-compulsory-purchase-and-the-crichel-down-rules-for-the-disposal-of-surplus-land-

necessitated 'sound evidence' to 'warrant taking someone's property from them',[178] *resonating with dissenting comments by Judge Scalia, in Kelo.[179]*.

Planning matters appear to be more political than legal. Especially when acquiring authorities are inextricably linked to the planning authority[180] and the executive. There is susceptibility to political lobbying.[181] The court has also held that 'lobbying is expected in a democratic society on the proviso that it is conducted properly and did not cause 'unfairness, bias or a perception thereof.'[182]

But due to the uncertainty of litigation[183], it appears more effective to lobby than pursue court processes which require access to decision makers and resources. In Haringey (HDV),[184] the local council leader was replaced and the scheme abandoned[185] following political pressure.[186] Although in *Horada,[187]* the court ruled in favour of the local community.

Preference for Negotiation

Government guidance[188] emphasises the importance of acquiring authorities to make reasonable initial offers about relocation, mitigation and accommodation works. There are other stipulations[189] and procurement rules, [190]as part of the CPO approval process[191] such as in 'estate regeneration'.[192]

Chapter 5

CPOs and Human rights

Human rights[193] are a fundamental consideration in the process of authorisation of CPOs.[194]

---

[178] Grafton Group(UK) v SOS for transport (2017) 1 W.L.R.373

[179] Kelo v City if New London Connecticut, [2004] USSC 3002; 542 U.S. 965 (28 September 2004)

[180] See objections against regeneration Minutes of Cabinet meeting held on 17 Dec 2018, https://moderngov.lambeth.gov.uk

[181] Broadview Energy Development V SOS DCLG (Broadview)

[182] Saira Kabir Sheikh QC, JPL 2013.13 Supp(just planning), OP91-OP104

[183] Order-of-the-Rt.-Hon.-Lord-Justice-Sales-26-09-2018.pdf, https://stophdv.com

[184] https://stophdv.com/

[185] https://www.theguardian.com/society/2018/jul/26/, relief-as-labour-confirms-scrapping-of-controversial-hdv-housing-project

[186] https://www.haringey.gov.uk/regeneration/haringey-development-vehicle

[187] [2016] EWCA Civ 16

[188] guidance-on-compulsory-purchase-and-the-crichel-down-rules-for-the-disposal-of-surplus-land

[189] s123 of Local Government Act 1972 and s233 of the TCPA 1990

[190] See Public contract regulations 2015

[191] Compulsory-purchase-process-and-the-crichel-down-rules-guidance https://www.gov.uk/government/publications/

[192] https://www.legislation.gov.uk/ukpga/1990/8/section/226

Among other requirements for CPOs, the human rights of those with interests in the land such as residents are a fundamental ingredient for authorisation of CPOs. As stipulated in the government guidance above which points to a need for compatibility with ECtHR.

Jurisdiction

The UK is a signatory to the ECHR[195]which incorporated the Human Rights Act fundamental freedoms into UK domestic law. The Act has to be read and given effect in compatibility with convention rights, by public authorities, through processes, decisions or impact thereof.

Therefore subject to the jurisdiction of ECtHR[196] and s3 of the HRA 1998.[197]

Section 4 of the HRA 1998 refers to 'declaration of compatibility of the law' but does not necessarily 'curtail the law'. Section 6 makes it unlawful for a public authority to act in a manner incompatible with convention rights and may apply to organisations which perform public functions[198].

Although UK courts do not have a requirement' to make identical decisions to the ECHR, the courts ought to 'take into account 'ECtHR decisions.[199]

Any person affected can bring a legal complaint but victims need to have standing under the CPO and the court can look at substance rather than form. A pressure group can be a victim if it shows that it's affected but it is for public authorities to show compatibility with ECHR rights although the complaint faces rejection if it is raised too late.[200]

States possess a margin of appreciation in implementation because housing is part of the social economic policy of a state. Which may require unique solutions unless there is a 'manifest unreasonable foundation'.[201] This may be

---

[193] See "Tesco Stores Limited v Secretary of State for the Environment and Others (Full Report)". *Journal of planning and environment law* (0307-4870), p. 581.

[194] guidance-on-compulsory-purchase-and-the-crichel-down-rules-for-the-disposal-of-surplus-land

[195] The Law of compulsory purchase, third edition, Guy Roots et al

[196] https://www.legislation.gov.uk/ukpga/1998/42/section/2

[197] *See nutshells, Human rights ;(state year?) See also HA1985-s7-Compulsory purchase/Human rights act guide to practitioners-Christopher Baker.*

[198] https://www.legislation.gov.uk/ukpga/1998/42/section/4

[199] https://www.legislation.gov.uk/ukpga/1998/42/section/4

[200] https://www.legislation.gov.uk/ukpga/1998/42/contents

[201] ECHR; https://www.echr.coe.int/Convention_ENG.pdf

interpreted differently from the perspective of the international convention rights, as highlighted by the UN Rapporteur on human rights.[202]

ECHR rights[203]

The rights protected by the ECHR are sixteen in total. Rights can be absolute, limited or qualified as indicated by Andrew Drzemczewski.[204] Property rights fall in the qualified category but are human rights no lesser than any other human rights.[205]

The most applicable human rights articles associated with CPOs include, *Art 2, Art 8, A1P1, Art 6, ART 14, Art 3, 10, 11, 13, 41 of the ECHR* incorporating the HRA 1998 , and international conventions.[206]

As a summary, Art 3[207] relates to inhuman and degrading treatment, Art 6 protects the right for a fair, expeditious and impartial process[208], Art 8 protects respect for a home and home environment[209], while Article 1 of the first protocol[210] , safeguards against unjustifiable, disproportionate interference in the peaceful and quite enjoyment of one's home and possessions[211]. Art 2 protects the right to life. Projects which threaten public health or public safety may trigger proceedings under article 2. ART 10 protects freedom of expression, Art 11 protects freedoms of association, ART13 deals with compensation and Art 41 specifies remedies. Article one of the first Protocol refers to principles of law and international law underlining the payment of compensation in as far as money can be compensation.[212]

Beyond the ECHR[213], the UK is party to the Universal Declaration of Human rights.[214] *The United Nations convention on economic, social and cultural rights invokes, 'the right of everyone to an adequate standard of living for himself and his family, including adequate housing.[215]*

---

[202] Special Rapporteur on extreme poverty and human rights; https://www.ohchr.orgExtremePoverty

[204] https://scholarlycommons.law.wlu.edu/cgi/

[205] https://www.echr.coe.int

[206] ECHR, https://www.echr.coe.int/Convention_ENG.pdf

[207] ECHR; https://www.echr.coe.int/Convention_ENG.pdf

[208] https://www.echr.coe.int

[209] https://www.echr.coe.int/Convention_ENG.pdf

[210] Referred to as A1P1 for brevity

[211] https://www.echr.coe.int/Convention_ENG.pdf

[212] https://www.echr.coe.int/Convention_ENG.pdf

[213] https://www.echr.coe.int/Convention_ENG.pdf

[214] http://www.un.org/en/universal-declaration-human-rights/

[215] https://www.ohchr.org/Documents/ProfessionalInterest/ccpr.pdf

Compensation is also covered under A1P1 making reference to principles of law and international law underlining the payment of compensation in as far as money can compensate the affected person/s.

There is however a distinction between a CPO where land is taken warranting compensation and imposition of restrictions per se, which amount to a taking or interfere with the use or enjoyment or ownership of the land and one where land is not taken. Balancing the need for compensation in both scenarios and public interest.

In addition, the European Social charter, protects health, family, property and against discrimination, among other rights.[216]

Chapter 6

Article 8 and CPOs

Article 8 of ECHR,[217] states that:
1. 'Everyone has the right to respect for his private and family life, his home and his correspondence.
2. There shall be no interference by a public authority with the exercise of this right except such as is in accordance with the law and is necessary in a democratic society in the interests of national security, public safety or the economic well-being of the country, for the prevention of disorder or crime, for the protection of health or morals, or for the protection of the rights and freedoms of others'.

Jurisdiction

Public authorities[218] as 'social' housing providers, attract the jurisdiction of HRA 1998 and Art 8 of HRA.[219] Residents affected by CPOs, could rely on Art 8(1), which reiterates that 'exercise of the CPO must be in accordance with the law'.[220]

In *Malone* where the issue involved determination of infringement of rights by surveillance, the court held that although this was consistent with domestic law,

---

[216] https://www.coe.int/european-social-charter

[217] https://www.echr.coe.int/Documents/Guide_Art_8_ENG.pdf

[218] Connors V UK(2005) 40 EHRR 9 'gypsies' removal from a locality was violation of art8

[219] R (weaver v London & Quadrant Housing Trust(2009) EWCA Civ 587

[220] Malone v UK (1984) ECHR 10

discretionary use and application by officers was 'arbitrary' and therefore incompatible with the ECHR.

Planning and public authorities possess opaque discretionary powers[221] susceptible to arbitrary use.[222] This is detrimental to individuals regarding decisions such as CPOs, demolition of homes, compensation, valuations and rehousing as indicated above. Hence, raising potential incompatibility with Art 8 if applied unlawfully where there are 'illegitimate aims' or disproportionate actions.[223]

Scope of Art 8

Art 8[224] protects 'respect for a home and against deprivation of a home by way of access or occupation. It safeguards the right to live without interference and intrusion in one's family or private life, correspondence as well as personal information being kept private and confidential. It requires a positive step from a public authority.

Definition of a home

'Home' as a general definition is a settled place where one lives, Including a home one has the intention to move to,[225] described as an 'autonomous concept' not based on domestic law categorisations.[226]

To engage Art 8 protection, there has to be a determination on facts relating to continuous links and rights, in a particular case which cannot be interfered with, unless there is a reasonable justification.[227]

There is no general right to housing under HRA or ECHR[228], except a respect for a home or justifiable interference of the peaceful and quiet enjoyment of one's home or possessions.

---

[221] Greg Brown & Sean Yeong Wei Chin (2013) Assessing the Effectiveness of Public Participation in Neighbourhood Planning, Planning Practice & Research, 28:5, 563-588, DOI: 10.1080/02697459.2013.820037

[222] Too-poor-to-play-children-in-social-housing-blocked-from-communal-playground, https://www.theguardian.com/cities/2019/mar/25/

[223] Lustig-Prean and Beckett v UK(1999)ECHR 71 relating to UK military ban on LBGT due to 'operational' issues

[224] ECHR

[225] Gillow v UK91986) ECHR 14
Donoghue V Poplar Housing association(2001)EWACA Civ 595

[226] https://www.echr.coe.int/Documents/Guide_Art_8_ENG.pdf

[227] https://www.echr.coe.int/Documents/Guide_Art_8_ENG.pdf

[228] https://www.echr.coe.int/Documents/Guide_Art_8_ENG.pdf

The state has a positive obligation to be proactive in regulating non state interference and to provide remedies against harassment of individuals in and around their home.[229]

The ECHR[230] classifies a home as meriting protection under the 'respect for a home' legal principle, extending to property where the complainant is not an owner, tenant, long term occupancy, a relative's house or a 'care' facility[231]. This may not apply to a 'home 'that one intends to build.[232]

Although Art 8[233] puts emphasis on a 'home' being non-transient or 'exceedingly 'short term', like a hotel room, in *Buckley v UK,* the notion of a home was not restricted to being 'lawfully established'.

Associated rights

Art 8 safeguards rights such as succession, contracts of parties and the protection of a positive duty to child integration since family law matters relate to a family home.[234] This is relevant to residents facing CPOs, who are not physically in occupation. Which may affect their re-housing, compensation or succession rights. This is not applicable to fiancées but extends to benefits or allowances indicating the 'respect for their family life'.[235]

Tenancies

Equally, there may be preconditions imposed on residents under CPO schemes, [236] whose occupation rights had ceased or those who are short term occupants. After displacing secure tenants[237] during the 'decanting' process.[238]

---

[229] Marckx x Belgium(1979)ECHR 2

[230] https://www.echr.coe.int/Documents/Convention_ENG.pdf

[231] https://www.echr.coe.int/Documents/Guide_Art_8_ENG.pdf

[232] Louizdou V Turkey(1996)ECHR 70

[233] https://www.echr.coe.int/Documents/Convention_ENG.pdf

[234] https://www.echr.coe.int/Documents/Convention_ENG.pdf

[235] https://www.echr.coe.int/Documents/Guide_Art_8_ENG.pdf

[236] http://estateregeneration.lambeth.gov.uk/key_guarantees#homeowners

[237] Part IV of HA 1985, amended by HA1988 and HA 96.

[238] Alice Belotti LSE Housing & Communities, Estate Regeneration and Community Impacts Challenges and lessons for social landlords, developers and local councils, Case report 99, March 2016

The significance is that, due to welfare cuts, sub renting or sharing homes is an affordable way to live[239] or work in some cities[240]. Although, there may not be agreements with the landlords, their 'homes' ought to have a level of protection beyond the narrow confines of statutory or contractual arrangements.[241] In circumstances where occupants do not fit the 'traditional' version of a 'home' that are affected by CPOs, as highlighted in *Chapman V UK*.[242] The concept of a home was expanded to cabins, bungalows stationed on land, irrespective of the lawfulness under national law as well as second homes.[243]

However, there may be limitations where there has been minimal occupation or weak links to the property to the extent that they are expunged. Sufficient nexus or occupation is necessary for recognition of a right to a home.

For example, a mere possibility of 'inheritance' may not give rise to a connection to a 'home' under Art 8.[244]. However, altering the terms of tenancy[245] was found to be interference in Art 8.[246]

But certainly the demolition of one's home or compulsory confiscation[247] attracts protection under Art 8.[248] Especially when there is compulsion to move, a clear interference in the respect to a home.[249]

Disrepair or blight

Also notable, in areas where the CPO processes are triggered, disrepair or neglect is a common feature[250] and appears incompatible with Art 8.[251] Disrepair has been found to be an infringement of Art 8, [252]after examining the existence of procedural guarantees to determine the margin of appreciation.

---

[239] Fenton, Alex. "Housing benefit reform and the spatial segregation of low-income households in London." (2011).

[240] Hamnett, Chris. "Moving the poor out of central London? The implications of the coalition government 2010 cuts to Housing Benefits." *Environment and Planning A* 42.12 (2010): 2809-2819.

[241] Michael Edwards (2016) The housing crisis and London, City, 20:2, 222-237, DOI: 10.1080/13604813.2016.1145947

[242] Chapman-v-united-kingdom-application-no-2723895

[243] https://www.echr.coe.int/Guide_Art_8_ENG.pdf

[244] https://www.echr.coe.int/Guide_Art_8_ENG.pdf

[245] Loretta Lees,**The Urban Injustices of New Labour's "New Urban Renewal": The Case of the Aylesbury Estate in London, 2013**

[246] (*Berger-Krall and Others v. Slovenia*, § 264);

[247] (*Aboufadda v. France* (Dec.));

[248] *Selçuk and Asker v. Turkey*, § 86; *Akdivar and Others v. Turkey* [GC], § 88; *Menteş and Others v. Turkey*, § 73).

[249] *Noack and Others v. Germany* (Dec.));

[250] Estate Regeneration and Community Impacts Challenges and lessons for social landlords, developers and local councils, Case report 99,Alice Belotti LSE Housing & Communities March 2016;
See also Save Cressingham gardens; Save Central Hill: @savewetburysw8

[251] (*Khamidov v. Russia*,

[252] *Novoseletskiy v. Ukraine*, §§ 84-88).

This is acutely relevant to 'victims' of CPOs[253] where the process is characterised with a lack of transparency, imbalance of resources, state self-interests or conflicts of interest due to decision makers being the acquiring party.[254]

Planning

Planning decisions leading to CPOs [255] are sometimes authorised by the same acquiring party, a manifest conflict of interest with detrimental impact.[256].

The *Kate Barker Report,* regarding the use of land for planning,[257] refers to 'planning decisions as policy decisions or expediency decisions', conducted in 'an anomalous manner subject to a degree of judicial review'.

CPOs processes, interfere with the respect for a home although that can be qualified under A1P1,[258] to allow a member state to maintain a 'degree of traditional, national or domestic approach', [259]If certain criteria are attached to the measures.[260]However, If the 'right in point is critical to the individual's 'enjoyment' of personal 'intimate' rights, the courts minimise the margin of appreciation.[261]

In_*Connors v. the United Kingdom,* the court held '*inter alia*', 'that the loss of one's home is a most extreme form of interference with the right to respect for the home'.

Private life

Private life is interpreted widely to include 'personal and physical integrity'[262]. The relevancy to CPOs is the excessive unjustifiable intrusion into people's lives culminating to eventual displacement.[263] Instigated through collection of

---

[253] Estate Regeneration and Community Impacts Challenges and lessons for social landlords, developers and local councils, Case report 99,Alice Belotti LSE Housing & Communities March 2016; See also Save Cressingham gardens;

[254]See inter alia Hackworth & Smith, 2001; Glynn, 2008; Lees et al., 2008; Shaw, 2008, argue that Stock transfer in London can be understood through the lens of state-led 'third-wave gentrification', a widespread phenomenon across British, North American and Australian cities.

[255] *Buckley v. the United Kingdom,* § 60);

[256]Siobhan O'Sullivan, et al. "Hearing the Voices of Children and Youth in Housing Estate Regeneration." *Children, Youth and Environments*, vol. 27, no. 3, 2017, pp. 1–15. *JSTOR*, www.jstor.org/27.3.0001.

[257] J.P.L 1570

[258] (*Howard v. the United Kingdom,*

[259] Alec Samuels,The planning process and judicial control: the case for better judicial involvement and control,J.P.L 1570

[260] *Noack and Others v. Germany* (dec.))

[261] (*Connors v. the United Kingdom,* § 82).

[262] X and Y v the Netherlands(1985) ECHR 4

[263] Jane Rendell (2017) 'Arry's Bar: condensing and displacing on the Aylesbury Estate, The Journal of Architecture, 22:3, 532-554, DOI: 10.1080/13602365.2017.1310125

personal data.[264] Residents may be vulnerable[265] with no access to independent advice or support. Such intrusion and 'disclosure' requires justification to avoid contravention of Art 8[266] especially where the acquiring authority is the 'intruding' party which arguably gains competitive negotiating, commercial and legal advantage.

Even providing information 'for census' purposes may be an interference of rights under Art 8 including surveys under the realm of Art 8 jurisdiction.[267] Intrusion in private life also includes loss of support networks in the locality which disrupts employment and professional associations[268]. The court has further found [269]the loss of employment for a 'breach of oath' to trigger Art 8, due to the impact it has on 'relationships, material well-being, family' and 'reputation'.

Fair process

CPO decisions and processes may not be understood or formalised during a disruptive protracted process for residents. Valuations, advance payments, negotiations for compensation or rehousing require specialist technical advice or access to financial resources.[270]

Valuations are determined largely by the acquiring authority with limited independent oversight and imposition of pre-conditions in case of a valuation dispute.[271].

Such measures should be conducted in a 'manner that respects the human dignity of affected persons and give respect to their home[272], giving appropriate weight to individual circumstances'.[273]

---

[264] *http://newmanfrancis.org/projects/westbury-lambeth/*

[265] https://www.ucl.ac.uk/engineering-exchange/sites/engineering-exchange/files/fact-sheet-health-and-wellbeing-social-housing.pdf

[266] As held in, Hilton V UK Application no,12015/86

[267] Z v Finland(1997) 25 EHHR 371

[268] Volkov Ukraine(21722/11) 2013 IRLR 480(ECtHR),

[269] Practical Law UK practice Note 8 835 5732

[270] Stuart Hodkinson, Chris Essen, (2015) "Grounding accumulation by dispossession in everyday life: The unjust geographies of urban regeneration under the Private Finance Initiative", International Journal of Law in the Built Environment, Vol. 7 Issue: 1, pp.72-91, https://doi.org/10.1108/IJLBE-01-2014-0007

[271] Estate Regeneration and Community Impacts Challenges and lessons for social landlords, developers and local councils, Case report 99,Alice Belotti LSE Housing & Communities March 2016; See also Save Cressingham gardens;
See inter alia Hackworth & Smith, 2001; Glynn, 2008; Lees et al., 2008; Shaw, 2008, argue that Stock transfer in London can be understood through the lens of state-led 'third-wave gentrification', a widespread phenomenon across British, North American and Australian cities.

[272] (*Rousk v. Sweden*, §§ 137-142).

[273] (*Gillow v. the United Kingdom*, §§ 56-58).

'Any person at risk of an interference of this magnitude should in principle be able to have the proportionality of the measure determined by an independent tribunal in the light of the relevant principles under Article 8.[274]

In *Connors V UK (2005) 40 EHRR9* it was held that the 'gypsies' removal from a locality was violation of Art 8 since the authority in question appeared to evade 'statutory' issues by making the 'applicant's wife' to sign a notice to quit', without due regard to 'respect for his home'.

Evictions

Art 8 also attracts protection against measures that lead to eviction.[275] CPO affected residents who are in effect 'removed' from their settled homes and community[276] are subjected to obscure broad, arbitrary and vague language, without access to independent legal advice[277].

Therefore, the duty to give reasons by a public authority, especially in CPO related matters, is crucial in securing one's rights.

As observed, *'Shakespeare's decadent, drunken and corpulently challenged knight, Falstaff, when pressed to give reasons to verify an obvious lie, robustly declined. He declared that if '... reasons were as plentiful as blackberries, I would give no man a reason upon compulsion'. 'But although Falstaff as a private individual was presumably within his rights to deny reasons, public authorities cannot be so cavalier. This is especially so where (as Lewison LJ recently observed in the Court of Appeal) 'the decision-maker is disagreeing with a considered and reasoned recommendation'.*[278]

Nuisance

Parties who may not possess direct proprietary interest may trigger 'proportionality', under Art 8, such as where a tree was felled into a neighbour's garden.[279] Applicable to parties affected by CPO construction nuisances, asbestos or contaminants.

[274] *(McCann v. the United Kingdom, § 50)*

[275] Donoghue, above

[276] Jane Rendell (2017) 'Arry's Bar: condensing and displacing on the Aylesbury Estate, The Journal of Architecture, 22:3, 532-554, DOI: 10.1080/13602365.2017.1310125

[277] Duty to give reasons:*https://www.lawgazette.co.uk/legal-updates/local-government-duty-to-give-reasons*

[278] Local government, duty to give reasons, ***https://www.lawgazette.co.uk***

[279] *Lane V The Royal Borough of Kensington and Chelsea London Borough Council(2013)EWHC 1320(QB)*

Although Art 8 does not offer an inherent protection of a 'clean environment' per se, planning decisions Interfere with people's home and family lives, therefore triggering Art 8 and A1P1[280].

Since the convention is considered to be 'a living instrument'[281], it should be interpreted to fit 'present day conditions'[282], to balance the rights of residents affected with a CPO with public authority actions, under art 8[283].

Among the effects of CPOs is the impact on longstanding communities[284] are compelled to move away from the locality, family and their support networks[285].

Yet the *'essential ingredient of a family is the right to live together, enjoy each other' company*[286] *and relationship development'*[287]. The 'notion of family life being an autonomous concept'.[288]

Chapter 7

Art 6

Art 6 (1) of the ECHR states that," In the determination of his civil rights and obligations or of any criminal charge against him, everyone is entitled to a fair and public hearing within a reasonable time by an independent and impartial tribunal established by law'.

Art 6(1) is applicable to property rights, privacy matters, internal hearings or processes in terms of procedural fairness, access to an independent tribunal or equality of arms.

Although Art 6 is not absolute[289] it refers to some procedural limits as acceptable without procedural guarantees at every stage but stresses access to a court with full jurisdiction[290].

---

280 *J.P.L 2010,3 298-309*

281 *Tyrer V UK*

282 *J.P.L 2010, 3 298-309*

283 https://www.echr.coe.int/Documents/Guide_Art_8_ENG.pdf

284 Paul Watt (2013) 'It's not for us', City, 17:1, 99-118, DOI: 10.1080/13604813.2012.754190

285 Tom Slater (2009) Missing Marcuse: On gentrification and displacement, City, 13:2-3, 292-311, DOI: 10.1080/13604810902982250

286 Olson v Sweden

287 Marckx v Belgium

288 Marckx v Belgium; https://www.echr.coe.int /Guide_Art_8_ENG.pdf

289 Ashingdale v UK(1985) 7 EHRR 528

290 Golder V UK (1975) EHRR 524

A key issue is whether a civil right in Art 6 is 'a private right as opposed to a public right'.[291] Since housing is consistent with a civil right in the context of ECHR and international conventions[292].

It's the civil arm of Art 6 that is applicable to CPOs requiring an identifiable issue over 'rights' that have jurisdiction in domestic law,[293] context, boundaries and application of that right.[294] This is due to competing interests between CPO parties, such as consultation,[295] a fair hearing or process and access to rehousing.[296]

Procedural fairness

Procedural fairness was an issue in *Ali V UK*[297], where an applicant should have been afforded access to a 'fair hearing before an independent and impartial tribunal'. In CPO matters, the decision making process is characteristically structurally advantageous or conducted by acquiring authorities' to secure their legal and financial interests against statutory standards of 'consultation'.[298]

In *Bokrosova V Lambeth*[299], it was held that Lambeth acted unlawfully. Stating that the process of consultation, *'must include sufficient reasons for the proposals to enable consultees to consider them, and respond to them intelligently; enough time must be given for that; and the consultation responses must be taken conscientiously into account when the decision is taken.... ensure public participation in the local authority's decision making process and ... in order for consultation to achieve that objective, it must fulfil basic minimum requirements'.* [300]

Nevertheless, the council still pursued the regeneration,[301] which questions the effectiveness of judicial review as a mechanism to challenge CPOs.

---

[291] Alec Samuels, The planning process and judicial control: the case for better judicial involvement and control,J.P.L 1570

[292] Kenna, P. (2008). Housing rights: positive duties and enforceable rights at the European Court of Human Rights. European Human Rights Law Review, 13(2), 193-208

[293] H V Belgium(1987) 8 EHH 123 and GEorgiadis V Greece

[294] Bentehm V Netherlands(1985 8 EHRR

[295] Bokrosova v LLB http://www.bailii.org/ew/cases/EWHC/Admin/2015/3386.html

[296] Begum v London Borough of Tower Hamlets(2003) UKHL 5

[297] Ali V UK(2016) 63 HRR 20,

[298] Alice Belotti, Estate regeneration and community impact, http://sticerd.lse.ac.uk/dps/case/cr/casereport99.pdf

[299] (2015)EWHC 3386(ADMIN)

[300] Citing *'one aspect of the Coughlan test'*

[301] https://savecressingham.wordpress.com/2016/12/21/residents-vow-to-fight-on-after-high-court-decision/

Pursuing legal action could theoretically attempt to meet the requirement of access to a 'fair and impartial hearing or tribunal'. However, prohibitive costs bar aggrieved residents from this course of action, especially leaseholders who risk cost orders[302], in addition to requirements for leave to be sought prior to commencement of legal proceedings.[303]

Parties with 'deep pockets' such as pubic bodies or property developers may unreasonably delay or deny their rights. Without the opportunity for the full circumstances ought to be fairly, diligently and impartially determined to prevent abuse of process or punitive penalties.[304]

In *Z and others V UK*[305], the court clarified that, *'the inability of applicants to sue the local authority flowed from the principles governing the substantive right of action in negligence as opposed to immunity'*. Hence, CPO affected residents will have Art 6 engaged if they were subjected to a 'blanket rule' that bars them from bringing civil actions against the acquiring authority.

National law and Art 6

Engagement of Art 6 requires a disputable implementation of national law, in a specific matter.[306] As held in *Lithgow,* where the 'nationalisation' of property, under a local Act,[307] was found to engage Art 6, after the applicants alleged a lack of statutory compensation.[308]

Property owners facing a CPO are entitled to statutory compensation under the s39 of the Land Compensation Act 1973. Where there are 'unreasonable or disproportionate' barriers, deriving from state laws, to a person's rights, Art 6 could be engaged. But the issue ought to be of a 'decisive' nature to the rights of an affected party[309], such as a home or business affected by a CPO leading to life changing intergenerational detriment hence engaging art 6.

In *Koning V Germany*[310], a civil right, under ECHR, was considered to be of 'substantive character' and defined 'autonomously' irrespective of the

---

[302] part-44-general-rules-about-costs,www.justice.gov.uk/courts/procedure-rules/c

[303] H V UK, Application no 11559/85

[304] Osman V UK(2000) 29 EHRR 245 (1998) ECHR 101 (1999) 1 LGRT 431

[305] Z and others V UK(2001) ECHRR 333, (2002) 34 EHRR 9

[306] Lithgow v UK

[307] Aircraft and Shipbuilding industries ACT 1977

[308] Practical Law Practice note 835 5732

[309] Practical Law Practice note 835 5732

characterisation under national law[311]. Similarly, in *Brugger V Austria*, it was held that the complainant was entitled to an oral 'hearing' especially that 'Judicial review' was not available as remedy in the local jurisdiction·

However, the absence of legal aid is an inherent disadvantage making it impossible for disenfranchised residents to challenge decisions. Especially leaseholders who risk substantial cost orders despite legal aid being necessary in civil proceedings.[312]

Proceedings such as valuations disputes should be determined by an independent tribunal [313] as opposed to mechanisms such as temporary appointments which could be incompatible with art 6[314]. Similarly, resolution should be in a reasonable time, consistent with individual circumstances of those concerned. There could be a breach such as In *Robins v UK*, there was a breach of Art 6 where there [315] was an unreasonable delay.

CPO processes characteristically take years in many cases to conclude, [316]with detrimental effect on residents on all areas of their lives. Acquiring authorities have extensive resources, unlike individuals, who are compelled to accept offers such as lower valuations that would otherwise be unacceptable.[317]

Imbalance of power and unfair proceedings

There is manifest imbalance of power and appearance of conflicts of interest in planning processes. A lack of fairness or 'equality of arms', procedural fairness or propriety.[318]

Arguably, in local authorities, planning committees, scrutiny committees or cabinet deliberations, decisions tend to favour the interest of the acquiring party, also the same Local Authority. Residents are accorded less time to argue their case or rebuttal of disputable facts.

---

[310] Koning V Germany(1978) 2 EHRR 170

[311] Practical law practice note,J.P.L, 2010,3, 298-309

[312] Stars and Chambers v Procurator-where appointment of a temporary sheriff was held to be incompatible with Art 6. One local authority proposed to appoint its own mechanisms of final arbitration

[313][313] See DCLG guidance; https://www.gov.uk/government/publications/compulsory-purchase-process-and-the-crichel-down-rules-guidance

[314]John Spencer, Maureen Spencer , Human Rights Nutcases,2 May 2002

[315] https://www.echr.coe.int/documents/guide_art_6_eng.pdf file:///T:/002-7866.pdf

[316] Dispossession the great social housing swindle : https://www.dispossessionfilm.com

[317] Stuart Hodkinson, Chris Essen, (2015) "Grounding accumulation by dispossession in everyday life: The unjust geographies of urban regeneration under the Private Finance Initiative", International Journal of Law in the Built Environment, Vol. 7 Issue: 1, pp.72-91, https://doi.org/10.1108/IJLBE-01-2014-0007

[318] R v (Wright v SOS for health and another(2009) UKHL 3

Possibly incompatible with Art 6 as held in *Borgers v Belgium*[319], where a defendant who couldn't hear or make responses to official arguments was said to have had his art 6 rights breached.[320] .In some cases, planning conditions are reportedly changed by the developers on the found after being accepted.[321]

Access to information

Accessibility to material information and the need to be 'heard' is critical to 'equality of arms'.[322] In the process of challenging or asserting their rights, information from public authorities is critical.

But FOI requests are protracted affairs and substantial information is not timely provided[323], or not provided[324], deducted or is in vague broad language. Access to hearings in public is not always guaranteed.[325]

Lack of independent reviews

Planning functions and permission processes conducted by local authorities [326]a ppear to be more political, are based on statutory grounds[327] and objections do not require a hearing, per se[328]. There is need for a fair balance between the rights of interests of the community and those of the applicant, to be presided over by an independent and impartial decision maker.

In *Tsfayo v UK (2007) ECHR 656*, the issue involved an applicants' renewal for housing and council tax which was rejected by the review board. The ECHR found that the board was not 'an independent tribunal' and the possibility of 'judicial review' was not a reprieve from the 'lack of independence' and included councillors.

Public authorities review their decisions by committees often staffed by councillors. The lack of a fair and impartial consideration would appear to engage Art 6. The imminent loss of a home, such as due to a CPO or a '*permit in breach of the applicable building regulations*' ought to be a serious *consideration* '[329], 'the loss of a home being one of the 'most extreme example.

---

[319] Borgers v Belgium(1993) 15 EHRR 92

[320] Practical law practice note public sector.

[321] https://www.theguardian.com/cities/2019/mar/25/too-poor-to-play-children-in-social-housing-blocked-from-communal-playground

[322] Feldbrugge V Netherlands(1986) 8 EHRR 425, see practice note above

[323] https://www.whatdotheyknow.com/request/asbestos_enquiry#incoming-1327131

[324] https://www.whatdotheyknow.com/request/somerleyton_road_steering_group_2321`11

[325] https://www.dailymail.co.uk/news/article-4656656/Kensington-councillor-DEFENDS-decision-meet-secret.html

[326] Bryan V UK(1995) 21 EHRR 342

[327] DCLG guidance

[328] R (Adlard V SOS for environment(2002) EWCA

There should be procedural measures and safeguards through regulation to protect parties' convention rights [330] with scrutiny placed on the protection of the residents' legitimate interests.[331]

Art 8 was held to be violated where there was no consideration of the impact of the applicant's personal circumstances.[332]Redeemably, it has been held that the vesting of land subject to a CPO *'cannot comply with Art.6 of the Convention, unless the courts have a jurisdiction to examine that decision on broad public law grounds'.*[333]

It could be 'unlawful if it were made for a purpose not recognised in the compulsory purchase order[334]*or unconnected with the reason for the grant of those powers. '*[335]

Restrictions on challenges

Planning policies, such as a CPO, infringe the rights of enjoyment of property and may reduce market value, contrary to Art 6, due to restrictions to challenge decisions. The Local Planning process is regarded as favourable to developers[336] and the right of appeal is limited to only applicants, although third parties can appeal to the inspector or pursue judicial review.

It is crucial[337]for objectors to *'have a fair crack of the whip'* by transparent access to pertinent material[338] and be able to have an opportunity to scrutinise evidence presented at a late stage in the process.[339]

Jeopardy lies with attitudes towards planning rights lead to detrimental decisions against CPO affected residents, such as where an actual 'local plan', by a Local Authority was not classified as a civil right.[340]

---

[329] (*Ivanova and Cherkezov v. Bulgaria*)

[330] (*Irina Smirnova v. Ukraine,* § 94).

[331] (*Orlić v. Croatia,* § 64; *Gladysheva v. Russia,* §§ 94-95; *Kryvitska and Kryvitskyy v. Ukraine,* § 50; *Andrey Medvedev v. Russia,* § 55)

[332] (*Ibid.,*§§ 49-62).

[333] Jonathan Ferris, 2010, Journal of Planning & Environment Law Compulsory purchase: is there a general right to judicial review to challenge the decision to vest land the subject of a confirmed compulsory purchase order?

[334] (*Grice v Dudley*8; *Capital Investments Ltd v Wednesfield Urban DC*9).

[335] *Congreve v Home Office*11; and *R. v Birmingham Licensing Committee Ex p. Kennedy*12).

[336] https://www.theguardian.com/cities/2015/jun/25/london-developers-viability-planning-affordable-social-housing-regeneration-oliver-wainwright

[337] Peter Harrison Qc, Glimpsed views of the legal land scape,

[338] R (on the application of Vieira) v Camden LBC

[339] R (on the application of Ashley) Secretary of state for communities and local government

[340] Bovis Homes V New Forest DC(2002) CIV 671

In some cases there are preconditions placed on valuation processes. Such as imposition of specific surveyors or appeal processes, which extinguish residents' rights without 'the proportionality of the measure being determined by an independent tribunal, which was held to infringe Article 8.[341]

Enforcement measures can be taken, through revocation or modification orders by the Secretary of State.[342] However, this also arguably raises questions as to whether there are fair mechanisms consistent with due process. Except later through the high court after the fact with substantial detrimental impact to affected applicants which would appear to be incompatible with Art.6.

Notably, the Supreme Court further held that although local authorities have the powers to revoke planning permission, they must take into account cost considerations.[343] This affects a well-intentioned local authority from asserting enforcement measures that would be beneficial to CPO affected residents. This further demonstrates the imbalance of power even in a judicial sense.

Where environmental or nuisance complaints are raised, during demolition or construction, some local authorities with 'confidential s106 agreements or other agreements, with developers, may have their impartiality or practical ability to enforce any planning regulations affected. Potentially leading to planning conditions being ignored after grant of planning permission.[344]

Chapter 8

Equal treatment

Equality[345] and fairness of treatment by those affected by CPOs, is critical to avoid breach of Art 14 in conjunction with Art 8. Article 14 has no free-standing existence in absence of other rights. As evident when in conjunction with Art 8, there was a breach of Art 14 when an 'occupant was prohibited from succeeding a tenancy after the death of his same-sex partner'.[346]

---

[341] '(*Kay and Others v. the United Kingdom,* § 74).

[342] Secretary of state

[343] **The Health and Safety Executive (Appellant) v Wolverhampton City Council (Respondent)**
[2012] UKSC 34 *On appeal from [2010] EWCA Civ 892*

[344] https://www.theguardian.com/cities/2019/mar/25/too-poor-to-play-children-in-social-housing-blocked-from-communal-playground

[345] https://www.echr.coe.int/Documents/Convention_ENG.pdf

Racial discrimination was also held to amount to a type of degrading treatment under Art 3, reiterated in the treaty of Rome as a free standing equal-treatment guarantee, although the UK has not signed that treaty. The race audit and the Institute of race relations[347], cite disparity in housing, valuations and disproportionate effects in estate in regeneration.[348]

National authorities have to pay close attention to the specific needs of minorities and those with protected characteristics. Which might include imposing certain conditions within reason albeit within certain limits.[349]

In *Chapman,* the court affirmed that restricting the use of caravans, has an impact on the applicants respect for their 'home'. This would be consistent with the residents affected by CPO who have cultural links or may be disadvantaged by being forced to areas whey they racial face discrimination.[350] As well as treating residents fairly and equally, especially on issues such as valuations of properties, rehousing and compensation, where racial minorities face a disproportionate detrimental impact on their lives.

In housing and estate regeneration, racial minorities face a disproportionate detrimental impact.[351] This is incompatible with the judgment in _Larkos v. Cyprus_ where 'the Court held that offering differential protection to tenants against eviction – according to whether they are renting state-owned property or renting from private landlords, entailed a violation of Article 14, taken in conjunction with Article 8, 'due to the unjustifiable difference of treatment'.

Beyond ECHR and the HRA 1998, international conventions bar discrimination and other human rights abuses. The universal declaration of human rights has moral authority [352] with given legal effect under the international convention on civil and political rights.[353] Applicable to housing are articles 23, 22, 3, 14, and 26, inter alia, ratified by the UK in 1976.[354]

---

346 (*Karner v. Austria,* §§ 41-43; *Kozak v. Poland,* § 99).
347 JESSICA PERERA,The London Clearances: Race, Housing and Policing, 2019
348 https://www.ethnicity-facts-figures.service.gov.uk/
349 (*Connors v. the United Kingdom,* § 84) (*Chapman v. the*

United Kingdom [GC], § 96; *Yordanova and Others v. Bulgaria,* §§ 129-130 /(*Codona v. the United Kingdom*

350 (*Chapman v. the United Kingdom* [GC], § 73).
351 JESSICA PERERA, The London Clearances: Race, Housing and Policing, 2019
352 http://www.un.org/en/universal-declaration-human-rights/
353 https://www.ohchr.org/en/professionalinterest/pages/ccpr.aspx
354 our-human-rights-work/monitoring-and-promoting-un-treaties, https://www.equalityhumanrights.com/en/

States are encouraged to implement adequate protections.[355] There is a positive obligation for a member state to cultivate appropriate safeguards as held in a case where lack of legal capacity, dispossession without meaningful participation, in the process or access to the final determination by the courts, was found to be a violation of art 8, having considered protection measures in national state law.[356] Emphasised in the Supreme Court[357], that the EA2010 provided further protection to a group of people who fall under 'the protected characteristics' category.

Public Sector Education Duty[358]

Under S149 EA2010, *'a public authority must, in the exercise of its functions, have due regard to the need to—eliminate discrimination, harassment, victimisation and any other conduct that is prohibited by or under this Act; advance equality of opportunity between persons who share a relevant protected characteristic and persons who do not share it; foster good relations between persons who share a relevant protected characteristic and persons who do not share the need to—tackle prejudice, and promote understanding. Compliance with the duties in this section may involve treating some persons more favourably than others; but that is not to be taken as permitting conduct that would otherwise be prohibited by or under this Act.'*

This is also stipulated under international convention on economic, social and cultural rights[359] with emphasis on art 10, 11 and 12 among othe*rs*.

CPO regeneration due to its interference in housing of settled communities creates adverse social impact highlighted by the UN the *rapporteur that, 'It was a British philosopher, Thomas Hobbes, who memorably claimed that without a social contract, life outside society would be "solitary, poor, nasty, brutish, and short." The risk is that if current policies do not change, this is the direction in which low-income earners and the poor are headed. Loneliness rates have soared and life expectancy rates have stalled in the United Kingdom, with the latest statistics showing a sharp drop in the annual improvement that has been*

---

[355] (*Stenegry and Adam v. France* (**Dec.**)).

[356] *Zehentner v. Austria,* §§ 63 and 65) / (*A.-M.V. v. Finland,* §§ 82-84 and 90).

[357] In Akerman –Livingston v Aster Communities Ltd(UKSC) 15,

[358] Public sector equality duty , EA2010

[359] https://www.ohchr.org

experienced every year since the records began, and an actual drop for certain groups'[360].

Which epitomises the adverse impact of such housing policies necessitating international human rights intervention. The practicality for residents to enforce obligations to timely or practically assist those affected, remains a distant or impossible prospect.

During CPO related construction, children face disruption in routine, living standards, ensuing noise, fumes and vibration which represents a real danger to their wellbeing. Such effects could be incompatible with the convention on children rights[361] due to the interference in the health and Protection[362] of Children.[363]

Chapter 9

Article 1 of the first protocol of the ECHR[364] and CPOs

A1P1 protects a land owner's or property interests with limitations.

A1P1 states that, *'every natural person or legal person is entitled to the peaceful enjoyment of his possessions and no one shall be deprived of his possessions except in the public interest and subject to the conditions provided for by law and by the general principles of international law.*

The preceding provisions shall not, however, in any way, impair the right of a state to enforce such laws as it deems necessary to control the use of property in accordance with the general interest or to secure the payment of taxes or other contributions or penalties'.

The main rules are that no interference with possessions, no deprivation of property, except in the public interest and that state control may only be justified legally in the general interest, infringed, where there is a 'legitimate justification'.

Art A1P1,[365]'covers all forms of property', does not limit ownership of 'possessions' such as 'physical goods' and is 'independent of national state

---

[360] https://www.ohchr.org

[361] https://www.loc.gov/law/help/child-rights/international-law.php

[362] https://www.nspcc.org.uk/preventing-abuse/child-protection,legal-definition-child-rights-law/legal-definition

[363] http://www.crae.org.uk/childrens-rights-the-law/laws-protecting-childrens-rights

[364] Referred to here as A1P1

[365] See Practical Law UK practice Note 8-385 5732

'definitions' but does not cover prospective possessions or 'future' possessions although it emphasises current or 'existing possessions.

A land owner's 'legitimate expectation' of enjoyment of property rights can be a basis for asserting A1P1 as held in *Pine Valley Developments,* where the applicant had bought land under the expectation of planning permission being approved.
This would be applicable to CPOs due to expectations of legal security of property interests, leases and secure tenancies whose curtailment would engage A1P1.[366]
As mirrored, in *Stretch*[367], where an *'applicant complained that he had been unjustly denied extension of a further 21 year term lease,*[368] [369]and the option granted by the local authority had been *'ultra vires'.*

The court stated that *'having regard to those considerations, there was a disproportionate interference with the applicant's peaceful enjoyment of his possessions and therefore, concludes that there has been a violation of Article 1 of Protocol No. 1 to the Convention'.*

The curtailment of resident's leases or secure agreements under a CPO could engage A1P1. In *Plant v Lambeth, above,* the court held that A1P1 had not been engaged in respect of secure tenants' rights. A potential 'legal claim' under A1P1 should merit consideration as a 'possession or asset', where a land owner has a 'legitimate expectation', that such a claim can be determined by a court.[370] Applicable to CPOs affected parties who have diametrically opposed interests with acquiring authorities.

Under A1P1, depriving someone of their property can only be 'justified' in exceptional circumstances, should 'reasonably' bear relation to market value of the property although the applicant needs to prove deprivation, not 'mere restrictions,[371] or temporary deprivation of use or enjoyment'. In *Lithgow et al,* deprivation of property was held to have happened where the 'state' confiscated property by way of a CPO.

In *Sporrong and Lonnroth*, the 'expropriation of building permits and building restrictions' enforcement, for specific 'durations' was held to be interference in

---

[366] Pine developments v Ireland(1992) 14 EHRR 319

[367] **Stretch v UK** *(Application no. 44277/98)*

[368] Practical Law UK practice Note 8-385 5732

[369] [2003] ECHR 320, (2004) 38 EHRR 12, [2003] NPC 125, [2004] 03 EG 100, [2003] 29 EG 118, [2004] 1 EGLR 11, *http://www.bailii.org/eu/cases/ECHR/2003/320.html*

[370] Pressos Compani Naviera v Belgium(1995) 2 EHHR 3010) , also see Practical Law UK practice note 8-385 5732

[371] See Practical Law UK practice Note 8-385 5732

the 'applicants' enjoyment of their land amounting to deprivation of property'[372]
.

Even a partial loss of a significant or 'substantial part' of a land owner's right, can lead to 'deprivation' without full 'expropriation'. This is consistent with CPO affected residents facing significant restrictions caused by CPOs, construction hazards like noise, fumes, vibration or contaminants or the restriction to sell[373].

In *James v UK*,[374] the court found that individuals with leases under the leasehold reform Act 1967, entitled to long leases who could purchase freeholds of their leases, at a defined statutory price, deprived freeholders of their property, due to the inability to 'sell the property or set the sale price'[375].

Paradoxically, this can benefit CPO affected residents[376] to disentangle them from the acquiring authority, although the acquiring authority would still have significant statutory powers to initiate a CPO, by citing other grounds such as 'control'. As opposed to 'seizure or forfeiture', which would not be deemed 'deprivation', a held in *Agosi V UK*[377]. Where the issue was *'seizure and forfeiture by customs of smuggled Kruegerrands'.*[378]

There is need to balance community interests and protection of individual's right to peaceful enjoyment of his home, in order to justify controlling the use of property 'in the 'general interest', affording significant latitude for acquiring authorities to use this as a defence in CPOs.[379]

Market value under A1P1

There could be violation where applicants are prevented from selling their properties at 'market value'. Such interference appears disproportionate since compensation should be 'reasonably related to the market value'. However, A1P1 does not guarantee a 'right to full compensation' in every situation since a margin of appreciation is allowed to the nation state in this respect.[380]

---

[372] Sporrong and Lonnroth(1982)5 EHHR 35

[373] Imrie, R., & Thomas, H. (1997). Law, Legal Struggles and Urban Regeneration: Rethinking the Relationships. *Urban Studies*, 34(9), 1401–1418. https://doi.org/10.1080/0042098975484

[374] James V UK(1986) 8 EHRR 123

[375] See Practical Law UK practice Note 8-385 5732

[376] See Cressigham Gardens in Lambeth

[377] Agosi v UK(1987) 9 EHRR1

[378] Practical Law UK practice Note 8-385 5732

[379] See R Plant V LLBC(cite full)

[380] See Lithgow and Practical Law UK Practice Note 8-385 5732

However, as highlighted by *Justice Scalia in Kelo*, the issue is beyond 'market value' per se since 'Market rate', in this context is disputed and described as 'a euphemism for imposing compensation' on an unwilling seller[381]. Where owners are compelled to sell to a specific party, at a specific time, at a price largely determined by the same interested party, the acquiring authority, who is the arbiter of the planning decisions, which is a manifest conflict of interest[382].

Residents buy properties without any CPO in mind with leases for 125 years. They envisaged this as a safety net both as a home and by capital accumulation. In areas like London, the Land Values have gone up significantly hence this being the main attraction for developers. The 'no scheme' principle is unrealistic since CPO affected areas face blight and disrepair which affected the market price.[383]

Therefore, the application of 'market price' or resemblance to 'market price' does not reflect the just, fair and equitable compensation for residents and their families.

Under A1P1, besides market price, compensation is also a relevant measure in assessing balance and the proportionate nature of the burden put on any CPO affected party.[384] *In James v UK* and in *the former king of Greece et al v Greece[385]*, it was held that compensation that does not 'reasonably' reflect the value of the property[386] could be deemed a 'disproportionate interference'[387].

John Pugh Smith, [388]humorously sums up the central concern for 'compulsorily purchased landowners', as 'timely adequate compensation'. Using humorous reference to especially for a 'welsh hill farmer',[389] where a central issue was the 'limitation period'.

The 'expeditious nature' and 'totality of compensation' is central to amicable resolutions of CPO related disputes. Acquiring authorities seek to offer less compensation through a deliberately slow process, while people's lives are on hold pending compensation[390].

---

[381] Guy Roots et al, 2nd edition

[382] Neil Gray Libby Porter, By Any Means Necessary: Urban Regeneration and the "State of Exception" in Glasgow's Commonwealth Games 2014

[383] Loretta Lees, Mara Ferreri, Resisting gentrification on its final frontiers: Learning from the Heygate Estate in London (1974–2013),Cities, Volume 57,2016,Pages 14-24, https://doi.org/10.1016/j.cities.2015.12.005.(http://www.sciencedirect.com

[384] Deborah Rook, Property and Human Rights, 2001

[385] Deborah Rook, Property Law and Human Rights, 2001

[386] Deborah Rook, Property Law and Human rights, 2001

[387] Holy Monasteries v Greece

[388] John Pugh –Smith, When is' enough ' legally enough, Encyclopaedia of Local government law bulletin,2015

[389] Saunders V Caerphilly CBC(2015)EWHC 1632 CH

THE COMPATIBILITY OF COMPULSORY PURCHASE ORDERS AND HUMAN RIGHTS © 2019 SHEMI LEIRA ESQUIRE

Acquiring authorities should 'take the lead' to avoid accusations of being 'unconscionable'[391]and employ ADR[392]. Litigation remains an expensive and unpredictable process.[393]As evidenced in a case where the court overturned the 'value of the scheme found to be £1.25millons more than the baseline scheme'.[394]

Chapter 10

CPO Compensation

Compensation is set by statute as highlighted in DCLG guidance[395]. Citing market value plus home loss payments and disbursements.[396]Disregarding, 'the value of the scheme' on the 'value of the land'.

But this does not cover the detrimental effects of being displaced from a settled community, fear and sense of powerlessness.[397]

Compensation assumes a willing seller without compulsion. Via monetary payment at the open market value of the land, *'in so far as money can do it' to put one in the same position as land had not been taken from him,...in so far as loss imposed on him in the public interest, but no greater'.[398]*

A government review culminated into law commission reports that were not implemented[399] leading to minimal changes.[400]

DCLG guidance also explains this contentious and complex area'[401] stating that, *'Compensation payable for the compulsory acquisition of an interest in land is based on the 'equivalence principle' (i.e. that the owner should be paid neither less nor more than their loss). The value of land taken is the amount which it*

---

[390] Alice Belotti, Estate regeneration and Community impact, LSE, 2016

[391] John Pugh –Smith, When is' enough ' legally enough, Encyclopaedia of Local government law bulletin,2015 , Citing Saunders V Caerphilly CBC(2015)EWHC 1632 CH

[392] Alternative dispute resolution

[393] Ridgeland properties Ltd V Bristol city council (2011) EWCA civ 649 ;(2011) R.V.R 232; (2011)5 WLUK 827 (CA) Civ Div.)

[394] Richard Harwood, J.P.L 2011,11,1498-1517

[395]compulsory-purchase-process-and-the-crichel-down-rules-guidance
https://www.gov.uk/government/publications

[396]https://assets.publishing.service.gov.uk/government

[397] Martine August, "It's all about power and you have none:" The marginalization of tenant resistance to mixed-income social housing redevelopment in Toronto, Canada,
Cities, Volume 57,2016,Pages 25-32, (http://www.sciencedirect.com

[398] Lord justice Scott in Horn v Sunderland corporation

[399] See urban renaissance report city university urban task force report, pg. 231,

[400] *Planning and Compulsory purchase Act 2004*

[401] DCLG guidance citing Part 1 Land compensation claims 1973

might be expected to realise if sold on the open market by a willing seller (Land Compensation Act 1961, section 5, rule 2), disregarding any effect on value of the scheme of the acquiring authority (known as the 'no scheme' principle); (see Land Compensation Act 1961, section 5, rule 5).

It is implied under A1P1 that compensation will be paid[402], but the legitimate public interest may 'justify less than the financial equivalent to what the claimant lost' based on the principle in *James*.[403] Or 'where rights to compensation are provided by statute', those 'provisions' must be interpreted so as to be compatible with HRA 1998'.[404]

A1P1 does not state how much compensation should be paid but states that *'the taking of property without any just compensation is justifiable only in exceptional circumstances'*. Compensation should be beyond pecuniary loss as summed up by Justice Scalia in *Kelo*.

Justice Scalia notes that, *'yes you are paying for it, but you are giving the money to somebody, who does not want the money, who wants to live in the house that she's lived in her whole life. That counts for nothing? 'What this lady wants is not money. No amount of money is going to satisfy her. Living in this house her whole life. She does not want to move'.*

That is the sense of deep injustice of the compulsory taking of homes occupied by settled communities. Especially in cases where there is no tangible or proven compelling public interest.

Beyond monetary compensation

Importantly, as part of restitution, occupiers should be entitled to rehousing[405] subject to certain criteria.[406]

For many longstanding residents affected by CPOS, especially those with young children, finding secure and affordable accommodation is one of the most formidable barriers they face. Many are compelled either to live on potentially hazardous and dangerous protracted construction sites, such as asbestos contaminated land, move into temporary accommodation or move out of the

---

[402] Guy Roots et al, 2nd edition

[403] James V UK, The Law of compulsory purchase, third edition, Guy Roots et al; *Thomas v Bridgend county council*,(2011), EWCA Civ 862, (2011) RVR 241

[404] Such as in *Thomas v Bridgend county council*,(2011), EWCA Civ 862, (2011) RVR 241, where the CA held that s19(3) of the Highway Act 1980, was incompatible with art 1 of the ECHR

[405] s.39 (1) Land Compensation Act 1973, as amended by para 6, Sch.15 Housing Act 2004

[406] *R v East Hertfordshire District Council ex p Smith (1990) 23 HLR 26; R v Bristol Corporation ex p Hendy [1974] 1 WLR 498.*

locality entirely, which causes a series of detrimental impacts in all areas of their lives.[407]

The new properties tend to take many years, to be build and are largely unaffordable. The new schemes such as shared ownerships, demote residents' property ownership interests, have stricter leases and diminish residents' equity, savings, home loss and disturbance.

Residents who exercise any rights to stay as tenants are subjected to intrusive means testing or inquiries into unrelated areas of their lives despite the injustice of having one's home confiscated by the same acquiring authority.[408].

In a widely reported case, after 'regeneration', children play grounds were segregated and 'poor doors'[409] depending on housing status incompatible with A1P1[410].

Compensation should proportionately reflect the public interest,[411] where land is taken, where there are imposed restrictions amounting to a taking due to the interference with the use, enjoyment or ownership of the land and one where land is not taken.

Proportionality

Under A1P1, proportionality emphasises a 'fair balance' between the public interest and the property interests of the owners.[412]

National authorities enjoy a wide margin of appreciation in determining 'the public or community interests, within the law' [413] by reflecting a need to be 'accessible, precise and foreseeable.[414]

Other factors determining fair balance include procedural safeguards of owner's property rights, the nature of the penalty applied, [415]the extent of interference,

---

[407] *PaulWatts,Its_not_for_us_Regeneration_the_2012_Olympics_and_the_gentrification_of_East_London_City_2013*, *http://www.academia.edu/6007431/;*
Zoe Williams, the real cost of regeneration,http://www.execreview.com/2017/07/the-real-cost-of-regeneration/

[408] *PaulWatts,Its_not_for_us_Regeneration_the_2012_Olympics_and_the_gentrification_of_East_London_City_2013*, *http://www.academia.edu/6007431/;*
Zoe Williams, the real cost of regenerationhttp://www.execreview.com

[409] https://www.newyorker.com/culture/cultural-comment/the-poor-door-and-the-glossy-reconfiguration-of-city-life

[410] /too-poor-to-play-children-in-social-housing-blocked-from-communal-playground
https://www.theguardian.com/cities/2019/mar/25

[411] As stated in Trailer and Marina(leven) v Sec.of State 2004

[412] See James V UK App No 8793/79 (A/98) (Official Case No)
[1986] ECHR 2 (Neutral Citation) ; James and ors v United Kingdom, Decision on Merits, App no 8793/79, B/81, 11th May 1984, European Commission on Human Rights (historical) [ECHR]

[413] Practical Law UK practice Note 8-835 57

[414] Hentrich V France(1994 18 EHRR 440 (1994)ECHR 29 Lithgow,

'duration,[416] the actual fault of the owner, its significance and the 'irrationality or arbitrary nature' of the statute.[417]

For CPO affected residents, 'proportionality in 'control cases' is not a basis for compensation but indicates a need for 'a fair balance' to be found.[418]
The interference *may only be 'justified legally in the general interest'.*

States are also allowed a *'margin of appreciation', in implementation of decisions, associated with legitimate objectives of public interest considerations[419] applicable to measures designed to 'achieve greater social justice'.*

In Tesco Stores Ltd v SOS[420] for Environment and Transport(2000), Sullivan J emphasised the need for a 'fair balance to be struck between the public interest' such as 'redevelopment' and the 'individual's right to a peaceful and quiet enjoyment of his possessions'.

Such interference ought to be 'proportionate and necessary' to meet the 'compelling case in the public interest' tests which 'reflects the necessary element of that balance'.[421]

An observation made in Chesterfield properties v Secretary of State,[422]that *'only another interest, a public interest, of greater force may override it'(In a CPO inspector's report,[423]objectors argued that 'as the Leaseholders' Article 1 and 8 rights have been breached, it is incumbent upon the Acquiring Authority to justify that breach in terms of proportionality.*

The objectors referred to, *'R (Clays Lane) v Housing Corporation, where, Maurice Kay J stated that 'the appropriate test of proportionality requires a balancing exercise' between 'a decision which is justified on the basis of a compelling case in the public interest as being reasonably necessary' may not be 'obligatorily the least intrusive of Convention rights.' Some 'leaseholders no longer have mortgages and many are no longer in employment, as a*

---

[415] International Transport Roth v HS(2002) EWCA Civ 158

[416] Sporrong and Lonnroth

[417] R(Kensall) v SOS for Environment(2003) Admin 2003

[418] See Practical Law UK practice Note 8-385 5732

[419] James v UK above

[420] J.P.L 2010,3 298-309

[421] Also see R (Clays Lane Housing cooperative ltd v Housing corp(2005),R (Pascoe v SOS(2007), R (Hall) v First SOS(2008) J.P.L 63 at 15

[422] Chesterfield Properties Plc v Secretary Of State For Environment & Ors [1997] EWHC Admin 709 (24th July, 1997), *http://www.bailii.org/ew/cases/EWHC/Admin/1997/709.html*
Cite as: 76 P & CR 117, (1997) 76 P & CR 117, [1997] EWHC Admin 709

[423] *CPO Report NPCU/CPO/A5840/74092 ,www.planningportal.gov.uk/planning inspectorate Page 73*

*consequence of the CPO they will be separated from their family and friends
and they will be unable to afford to return to the estate'.*

The inspector agreed, that, *'Paragraph 12 of the Guidance states that an
acquiring authority should be sure that the purposes for which the compulsory
purchase order is made justify interfering with the human rights of those with
an interest in the land affected. They would need to invest considerable
personal resources in addition to any compensation they would receive for their
properties, the CPO would not only deprive them of their dwelling but also their
financial security.*

*If they chose not to pursue this option, they would inevitably need to leave the
area and this would have implications for their family life, including the lives of
those dependant on the.... together with the failure of the scheme to fully
achieve the social, economic and environmental well-being.*

*The interference with human rights would not be proportionate having regard
to the level. The public benefits that the scheme would bring... a compelling
case in the public interest has not been proved'.*

Hence emphasising human rights as a fulcrum of CPOs schemes not simply a
peripheral matter.

Interference

Tax enforcement is a reason where a margin of appreciation is applicable. A
state has a right to enforce laws deemed necessary to control use of property in
accordance with the general interest to secure payment of taxes, penalties or
lawful regulations. As long as the power is exercised 'rationally and
'proportionately', such as regulation of a sex shop.[424].

In *Davies*, the court held that A1P1 was engaged, in the 'absence of fair
compensation' thereby breaching the need for striking a 'fair balance' between
the public interest and the 'van owners'.

However, there was a 'wide margin of appreciation', since the council had an
'appeal system, was 'reasonable' and was 'proportionate'.

The court could find a breach, where there is a discretionary, unfair procedure
creating an excessive burden born by the applicant. The court can further

---

[424] *Belfast CC v Miss Behavin' Ltd,*([2007] WLR 1420, [2007] 1 WLR 1420, [2007] 3 All ER 1007, [2007]
UKHL 19, *http://www.bailii.org/uk/cases/UKHL/2007/19.html*

intervene in the absence of a reasonable justification for interference with property rights.[425]

Affirming that natural or legal persons can only be deprived of property, subject to conditions provided by law, the general principles of international law or other interests,[426] like 'contributory or non-contributory' state benefits.[427]

The fair practice would be to offset any outstanding payments with compensation since complaints or appeals may depend on residents' securing evidence from acquiring authorities.

Home environment

Interference has to be proportionate, with, 'a positive obligation on contracting states' to ensure proportionality with the stated aim. For instance, environmental pollution could interfere with private life and deprive a personal enjoyment of amenities associated with one's home. The court concluded that noise pollution violated articles 8 and 13 of ECtHR[428]. Although state parties should consider environmental protection within a margin of appreciation.

Interference may also affect a person's wellbeing and prevent them from enjoying their homes, family life and adversely affecting their health. Noise from a nuclear plant was found to have affected living conditions although it was held as beneficial.

However, despite specific or overt protection of a 'healthy environment,[429] if there is a 'serious' detriment to the persons concerned or a direct nexus to the cause, a complaint may arise under Art 8, to determine[430] state actions or its failure to effect measures necessary to prevent harmful activity.

Emphasis is placed on the need for a causal link to be established as opposed to prospective harm depending on the repetitive nature of the negative activity.[431] Prevention should be effected before any harm or interference in the peaceful enjoyment for affected faced with CPOs parties.

---

[425] R Mott v Environment Agency(2018) UKSC 10)

[426] Beyeler v Italy(2001) 33 EHRR 52

[427] Stec v UK(2005)41 EHRR SE18

[428] https://www.echr.coe.int/Documents/Convention

[429] *Kyrtatos v Greece*

[430] (*Hatton and Others v. the United Kingdom* [GC], § 96; *Moreno Gómez v. Spain,* § 53)

[431] *Fadeyeva v. Russia,* § 69.

It's not the general deterioration of the environment", per se, but harmful effects that would be disproportionate to the accepted standards consistent with living in a modern metropolitan areas.[432]

In reaching its decision regarding a breach under Art 8, associated with pollution, the courts consider process and substance.[433] Paying due regard to any vague or overbroad interference without reasoned decisions or processes, any shortcomings in a state's obligation or whether the right balance has been struck between the resident and other interested or parties.[434]

Such measures need not include extensive reports but include professional assessments to determine the injurious consequences of construction activities. However, a decision may be made in the absence of such information, [435] if a fair balance between parties exists.

Additionally, a failure to rehouse residents during demolition, excavation, redevelopment, could violate Art 8,[436] due to a failure to protect their health and wellbeing.[437]

Protective measures include regulatory and administrative mechanisms. Paradoxically, the court confines itself to 'respect for a home'. The wisdom of such a decision needs to be closely examined.[438]

Courts have been creative in decisions that had the effect of remedying environmental detriments to residents by finding violation to a 'home'.[439]

Such as requiring transparency where residents living at a dangerous site with sodium cyanide or in proximity to hazardous effects were not provided access to information or 'conclusions' of the study to permit such a scheme.[440]

---

[432] . (*Asselbourg and Others v. Luxembourg* (Dec.)).
(*Martínez Martínez and Pino Manzano v. Spain*, § 42) (*Hardy and Maile v. the United Kingdom*

[433] (*Hatton and Others v. the United Kingdom* [GC], § 99).

[434] *Moreno Gómez v. Spain*, § 55). (*Fadeyeva v. Russia*, § 93; *Hardy and Maile v. the United Kingdom*, § 218

[435] *Hatton and Others v. the United Kingdom* [GC], § 128)

[436] *Fadeyeva v. Russia*, § 133

[437] *Tătar v. Romania*, § 88).

[438] (*Hatton and Others v. the United Kingdom* [GC], §§ 100 and 122),

[439] *López Ostra v. Spain*, §§ 56-58, *Moreno Gómez v. Spain*, § 61. *Di Sarno and Others v. Italy*, § 112).in (Giacomelli v. Italy, §

83),

[440] Hatton and Others v. the United Kingdom [GC] (§ 120),

This is consistent with the experiences of many residents living in CPO affected areas, where there is a lack of independent 'impact environmental and equality impact assessments.

As reflected in the case of _Giacomelli v. Italy,_ where *the 'Court found a violation in the absence of a prior environmental-impact assessment and the failure to suspend the activities of a plant generating toxic emissions close to a residential area'.*

Crucially, environmental impact damages may be linked to actual loss. Applicants, who lived near Heathrow,[441] were subjected to noise nuisance which affected property valuation but there was no evidence to suggest that the value of the applicants' property diminished or was unsalable.[442]

Similarly, bad housing conditions, disrepair or 'blight' during CPOs[443], may breach quiet enjoyment and Art 8 relating to 'respect for a home'[444].

However, despite statutory obligations[445], there doubts about local authorities' willingness to enforce their own statutory liability or culpability. Necessitating a need for Art 8 intervention, where there are unfit conditions but no adequate remedy.[446]

CPOs, right to buy and A1P1

R Plant v LLBC[447] highlights issues facing secure tenants faced with a CPO and interference in their right to buy under A1P1.

A central issue was whether A1P1 was engaged and breached by the council's decision. The court held that A1P1 was not applicable to the council's cabinet decision, concluding that, *'A1P1 is not engaged and indistinguishable from other authorities.*[448] Which the claimant alleged to have been breached due to interference with S118 of HA 1985, right to buy and S84 (1) rights, which prevent the court from issuing a possession order on such a property. Except on legal grounds in 'schedule 2' of the Act and other provisional requirements.[449]

---

[441] Hatton and Others v. the United Kingdom [GC] (§ 120),

[442] . However, a settlement was reached in one case in respect of Art 8, 13 and A1P1.

[443] Demolition or refurbishment of social housing?, https://www.ucl.ac.uk/engineering-exchange/research-projects, 2018

[444] https://www.echr.coe.int/Documents/Guide_Art_8_ENG.pdf

[445] Housing/repairs-in-rented-housing/disrepair-what-are-your-options-if-you-are-a-social-housing-tenant/disrepair-what-are-the-landlord-s-responsibilities, /https://www.citizensadvice.org.uk/

[446] HA1985 s604,

[447] *R Plant v LLBC, [2016] EWHC 3324 (Admin)*

[448] _Kay v Lambeth LBC [2005] QB 352 and Austin v Southwark LBC [2010] HLR 1'._

[449] *R Plant v LLB [2016] EWHC 3324 (Admin)*

Noting that *'if engaged, it need only be considered in relation to the statutory right to buy when the authority commences County Court proceedings to obtain an order for possession of a particular home'*.

The court appeared to restrict this to the fact that the claimant had not already exercised his right to buy. However, the existence of that option and its removal appeared to interfere in the claimant's property rights, engaging A1P1.

Nevertheless, the court appeared to acknowledge that A1P1 was engaged to the point when steps would be taken to revoke it. Stating that, *'If, contrary to the clear view I have reached, I had concluded that A1P1 was engaged in LLBC's decision, reached on 21 March 2016....the issue of whether it was breached would have been a matter for the Court to determine.'*[450]
Inviting the question as to when the right time or forum would be for the Claimant to enforce his rights under A1P1.

For CPO affected secure tenants the court appears to have acknowledged their rights, if they chose to move away. They would be 'secure tenants being provided with new secure tenancies if they decide to move elsewhere, but not if they wish to be rehoused in a new home on their current location, in which case they would only be granted an assured tenancy.   The unfortunate refusal to appeal closed down testing the decision in higher courts.

Chapter 11

Art 11[451]

Article 11 – states that:
1. 'Everyone has the right to freedom of peaceful assembly and to freedom of association with others, including the right to form and to join trade unions for the protection of his interests.
2. No restrictions shall be placed on the exercise of these rights other than such as are prescribed by law and are necessary in a democratic society in the interests of national security or public safety, for the prevention of disorder or crime, for the protection of health or morals or for the protection of the rights and freedoms of others. This Article shall not prevent the imposition of lawful restrictions on the exercise of these rights by members of the armed forces, of the police or of the administration of the State'[452].

---

[450] Citing *Belfast City Council v Miss Behavin' Ltd [2007] 1 WLR 1420* at paragraphs 13 to 15)'.

[451] https://www.echr.coe.int/LibraryDocs/DG2/HRFILES/DG2-EN-HRFILES-11(1998).pdf
[452] https://www.echr.coe.int/Documents/Convention_ENG.pdf

Limitations can only be placed on these rights for public policy grounds.[453] The relevance to CPOs affected parties is manifested in how local authorities influence and diminish resident's ability to meet, organise and express themselves, during the process of consultation or challenging the entire process of acquisition.

There are traditionally elected bodies known as TRAs.[454]In some cases, residents' elected groups have been 'suspended' to stop effective, representative association without influence or manipulation by the authorities concerned.

TRAs tend to be more effective and organised in challenging Local Authority's decisions but there are examples where such associations have been either suspended or marginalised,[455] residents' advocates complained of being singled out, targeted or victimised.[456]

Such actions have a chilling effect on residents' ability to scrutinise or challenge the decisions, actions of such public bodies, [457]therefore jeopardising residents' ability to safeguard their human rights[458].

In many reported areas, there is no evidence to justify curtailment of those rights in the context of CPOs[459].

Chapter 12

Art 11[460]

'Freedom of assembly and association
1.   'Everyone has the right to freedom of peaceful assembly and to freedom of association with others, including the right to form and to join trade unions for the protection of his interests.
2.   No restrictions shall be placed on the exercise of these rights other than such as are prescribed by law and are necessary in a democratic society in the interests of national security or public safety, for the

---

453 Observer and the Guardian v the United Kingdom (1991)

454 Tenants and Residents Associations

455https://lambethleaseholders.wordpress.com

456https://newsfromcrystalpalace.wordpress.com/2016/10/26/leaseholders-chairman-quits-amid-council-bullying-claims-green-party-councilor-says-siege-mentality-exists-in-lambeth/

457 http://lambeth.network/wp-content/uploads/2016/04/LCTC-Res-Engmt-Survey.pdf

458 https://www.equalityhumanrights.com/en/human-rights-act/article-11-freedom-assembly-and-association

459what-are-human-rights/human-rights-act/article-11-right-protest, https://www.libertyhumanrights.org.uk/human-rights/

460 https://www.echr.coe.int/LibraryDocs/DG2/HRFILES/DG2-EN-HRFILES-11(1998).pdf

prevention of disorder or crime, for the protection of health or morals or for the protection of the rights and freedoms of others….."'''

Limitations can only be placed on these rights, for public policy grounds.[461] The specific relevance to CPOs affected parties is manifested in how local authorities influence and diminish resident's ability to meet, organise and express themselves, during the process of challenging the entire process of acquisition. On housing estates for example, there are traditionally elected bodies known as TRAs[462]. In some cases residents' elected groups have been 'suspended' to dissuade, hinder or stop effective, representative and free association without influence or manipulation by the authorities concerned[463].

Tenants Residents Associations tend to be more effective, vocal and organised in challenging Local Authority's decisions but there are examples where such associations have been suspended, marginalised or ignored[464]. Or where resident's advocates or leadership have complained of being singled out, targeted or victimised[465].

Such actions have a chilling effect on resident's ability to question, analyse, scrutinise and challenge the decisions or actions of such public bodies[466], jeopardising residents' ability to safeguard their property rights and other human rights[467].

There is no evidence to justify curtailment of those rights[468], in the context of CPO processes.

Article 2 of ECHR[469]

"1. *Everyone's right to life shall be protected by law. No one shall be deprived of his life intentionally save in the execution of a sentence of a court following his conviction of a crime for which this penalty is provided by law.*

---

[461] Observer and the Guardian v the United Kingdom (1991)

[462] Tenants and Residents Associations

[463] housing-scandal-one-council-to-choose-who-represents-tenants-and-leaseholders-on-new-residents-assembly/https://newsfromcrystalpalace.wordpress.com

[464] https://lambethleaseholders.wordpress.com/

[465] https://newsfromcrystalpalace.wordpress.com/2016/10/26/leaseholders-chairman-quits-amid-council-bullying-claims-green-party-councilor-says-siege-mentality-exists-in-lambeth/

[466] http://lambeth.network/wp-content/uploads/2016/04/LCTC-Res-Engmt-Survey.pdf

[467] https://www.equalityhumanrights.com/en/human-rights-act/article-11-freedom-assembly-and-association

[468] https://www.libertyhumanrights.org.uk/human-rights/what-are-human-rights/human-rights-act/article-11-right-protest

[469] https://www.echr.coe.int/Documents/Convention_ENG.pdf

Art 2 protects life with defences specified in Art 2(2)[470]. Governments should protect citizens from the excess, failures or illegalities of industry which among other detriments may harm the public.[471] As highlighted in *Oneryildiz v Turkey, where there was a lack of protection for citizens living near a garbage bin.[472]*.

International law may be applicable through the environmental regulation sphere,[473] in convergence with Art 8 of ECHR which asserts respect for the home and protects family life.[474]

Art 2 is relevant due to the adverse impact on residents' well-being, health and public safety during protracted large scale construction with potentially harmful effects of vibration, fumes, noise, asbestos contamination,[475] that residents are subjected to, for prolonged periods which is clearly incompatible with Art2. Enforcement remains a formidable impediment due to lack of resources and imbalance of power.

Chapter 12

Impact on Children

The use of CPOs to demolish and acquire social housing, affects children in multifaceted ways. Such as the dislocation from their support systems, local schools, faith or community centres and immediate or long term adverse impact on their health. There are reports of segregation on the basis of tenure at play centres, which deprive children of their basic needs[476] and has underlying racial connotations due to income disparities.[477]

---

[470] https://www.echr.coe.int/Documents/Convention_ENG.pdf

[471] Dimitri Xenos, Asserting the Right to life (Article 2, ECHR) in the Context of Industry 8 German L.J. 231 (2007)

[472] Oneryildiz v. Turkey, 2004-XII Eur. Ct. HR 79, First, Do No Harm: Human Rights and Efforts to Combat Climate Change 38 Ga. J. Int'l & Comp. L. 593 (2009-2010

[473] Human Rights and Criminal Justice Applied to Legal Persons. Protection and Liability of Private and Public Juristic Entities under the ICCPR, ECHR, ACHR and AFChHPR P.H.P.H.M.C. van Kempen

[474] Kristof Hectors, Chartering of Environmental Protection: Exploring the Boundaries of Environmental Protection as Human Right, 17 Eur. Energy & Envtl. L. Rev. 165 (2008)

[475] John L Adgate, Sook Ja Cho, Bruce H Alexander, Gurmurthy Ramachandran, Katherine K Raleigh Jean Johnson,, Rita B Messing, A L Williams, James Kelly & Gregory C Pratt
Modelling community asbestos exposure near a vermiculite processing facility: Impact of human activities on cumulative exposure, Journal Of Exposure Science And Environmental Epidemiology
2011/02/23

[476] https://www.theguardian.com/cities/2019/mar/25/too-poor-to-play-children-in-social-housing-blocked-from-communal-playground

[477] The London clearances, Race, Housing and Policing, http://www.irr.org.uk/publications/issues/the-london-clearances-race-housing-and-policing/

But CPOs and the impact on children is part of wider social policy, since some local authorities claim that estate regeneration is a consequence of the 'austerity policy.[478]'

Although that does not reflect the totality of the issue as highlighted by the Institute of Race Relations which delves into the more nuanced and complex interplay of race, housing and policing.[479] Which may require an entire book.

As Professor Philip Alston, observes, a wealthy country with the 'fifth' largest economy in the world should not be *patently unjust... that so many people are living in poverty'[480]. Pointing out that the Institute for Fiscal Studies foresees, 'a 7% rise in child poverty between 2015 and 2022, and various sources predict child poverty rates as high as 40'.*

Observing that *'almost one in every two children to be poor in twenty-first century Britain is not just a disgrace, but a social calamity and an economic disaster, all rolled into one'. There is evidence from the Equality and Human Rights Commission which predicts that 'another 1.5 million more children will fall into poverty between 2010 and 2021/22 as a result of the changes to benefits and taxes, a 10% increase from 31% to 41%,'according to Professor Philip Alston. Further indicating that the Social Metrics Commission, states that 'almost a third of children in the UK live in poverty. After years of progress, child poverty is rising again, and expected to continue increasing sharply in the coming years.'*

Prof. Alston concludes that, *'It was a British philosopher, Thomas Hobbes, who claimed that without a social contract, life outside society would be "solitary, poor, nasty, brutish, and short.*

The risk is that if current policies do not change, this is the direction in which low-income earners and the poor are headed. Loneliness, life expectancy rates have stalled in the United Kingdom' while 'at the same time many of the public places and institutions that previously brought communities together, such as libraries, community and recreation centres and public parks, have been steadily dismantled or undermined'.[481]

---

[478] Broughton, K., Berkeley, N., & Jarvis, D. (2013). Neighbourhood regeneration in an era of austerity? Transferable lessons from the case of Braunstone, Leicester. Journal of Urban Regeneration and Renewal, 6(4), 381-393

[479]The London Clearances, race, housing and policing http://www.irr.org.uk

[480] Professor Philip Alston, United Nations Special Rapporteur on extreme poverty and human rights

[481] Report from UNRA rapporteur on human rights, by Professor Philip Alston, United Nations Special Rapporteur on extreme poverty and human rights https://www.ohchr.org/Documents/Issues/Poverty/EOM_GB_16Nov2018.pdf

Such effects, on children would be incompatible with Children Human rights under international law, Art 8 of ECHR, Art 2 and the international convention on the rights of the child.[482]

At this point, it is prudent to analyse the protective measures that can be deployed by those affected. Such as judicial review, inter alia.

Chapter 13

Judicial review and CPOs

The ability for aggrieved parties to seek judicial review is crucial to CPO affected parties. Peter Harrison QC, citing *Barker*,[483] noted that the court of appeal indicated that planning issues are not merely *'bilateral'* matters since the impact is widespread, therefore those affected may bring legal proceedings.[484]

Third parties or a 'non-party to an obligation'[485] may seek a declaration through judicial review. An example of such an issue would be interpretation of s106 obligation'[486] or quashing the decision of the LPA[487] to allow a basement enlargement for a pool.[488]

Ultimately, the deciding body can reinstate the initial position after 'curing' the initial procedural defects with the same outcome. As such, judicial review, as an effective mechanism, is perhaps one of largely tactical delays to the CPO implementation.[489]

In *Bokrosova v LBL Lambeth,* the issues were unlawful consultation, in breach of s105 HA and other common law requirements, although the judge quashed the decision, the local authority proceeded with the CPO process after it 'restarted' the 'consultation', linked[490] to Plant,[491] where the court denied judicial review and refused permission to appeal.

---

482 Convention on the right of the child, https://www.ohchr.org
483 2012(EWCA) Civ 61021
484 Peter Harrison QC, Glimpsed view of the landscape, J.P.L 2012
485 Milebush properties ltd v Tameside MBC(2011) EWCA Civ 270
486 J.P.L OP121
487 Local Planning Authority
488 J.P.L 2011, OP94-122
489 See Borksova and R v(Plant) against London Borough of Lambeth
490 Save Cressingham gardens campaign, https://savecressingham.wordpress.com/
491 See R (plant) V LBLambeth

However, in *Horada, above,* judicial review provided small businesses in Shepherds Bush Market, with a potentially permanent relief against a CPO. The notable difference is a residential CPO and business owners.

Despite the lack of durable effectiveness of judicial review, contracting parties have responsibilities to comply with subsequent damages awarded to the complainant.

There are also legitimate questions about 'a general right of judicial review' in addressing complex issues such as 'decisions to vest land' which is a 'subject of a confirmed compulsory order.'[492] To challenge the AA[493] from vesting a CPO, the objector would have to demonstrate, that the 'AA's rights are against good conscience'.

This is highlighted in *Simpson*[494], *where Lord Evershed indicates that one would have to show 'one or both' 'bad faith, misconduct, abuse of power, alteration of a position', omission, commission through bad faith that negated a belief that there would be a speedy acquisition of ones' land. In effect a creation of an unfair position because of the 'long period' that has 'elapsed'.*

There are strict timelines of bringing a JR in general hinder successful actions due to the enormity of the task of collecting evidence, lack of resources and identifying effective legal representation.[495]

Therefore, the notion of fairness, parity of parties and access to an impartial tribunal, consistent with Art 6 appears to be largely unachievable for many communities faced with a CPO.

Considering the imbalance of power and potential risk to human health, it would be assumed that the balance should be weighted in favour of protecting risk to health such as asbestos as opposed to administrative matters, per se.

This brings into question the relevance of the *'Wednesbury principle'*.[496] Observers point to the absence of human rights 'engagement', which triggers the consideration of the conventional principle of irrationality, unreasonableness or breach of a statute'. Depriving the applicants of the consideration of

---

[492] Jonathan Ferris, Journal of Planning & Environmental review, 2010

[493] Acquiring authority

[494] Simpsons Motor Sales(London) ltd V Hendon Copr(No.1) highlighted in J.P.L 2010,552-556

[495] Council-wins-Haringey-development-vehicle-judicial-review, https://www.insidehousing.co.uk ; Anna Minton, "The Price of Regeneration," *Places Journal*, September 2018.

[496] Peiris, G. (1987). Wednesbury Unreasonableness: The Expanding Canvas. *The Cambridge Law Journal, 46*(1), 53-82. doi:10.1017/S0008197300113613; Veena Srirangham 4 ISLRev 46 (2016-2017), The Difference in Kind- Proportionality and Wednesbury

'proportionality' which attracts more scrutiny of the public interest through the prism of 'social need' when human rights are 'engaged'.[497]

The relevance of judicial review for applicants faced with the expropriation of their homes remains a difficult legal hurdle. This should engage an extensive investigation of Art 6, as highlighted in *Alconbury*[498]where Tuckley J firmly challenged the notion of the minster being 'impartial, independent and a non-party to his own cause'.[499]

Hence raising doubts about the efficacy of judicial review as an effective mechanism.

Chapter 14

Remedies

ARTICLE 13

Art 13 , states that , 'Everyone whose rights and freedoms as set forth in this Convention are violated shall have an effective remedy before a national authority notwithstanding that the violation has been committed by persons acting in an official capacity'.

The remedy depends on the seriousness of the act which determines the quantification of the damages.

---

[497] Alec Samuels, The planning process and judicial control: the case for better judicial involvement and control,J.P.L 1570

[498] Alconbury [2001] UKHL 23; [2001] 2 All ER 929 (9th May, 2001)

[499] Alec Samuels, The planning process and judicial control: the case for better judicial involvement and control,J.P.L 2007, 1570-1577

Article 13 is not incorporated in HRA1998 but lays out principles which can be effective as a remedy such as the seriousness of the act being proportionate to damages. For instance ignoring torture was tantamount to undermining the effectiveness of any available remedy to the applicant, due to the use of the police complaints procedure which was not considered to be an adequate remedy under Art 13.

Article 41[500]

Article 41 refers to just satisfaction' to the injured party and a causal link between loss and violation including speedier proceedings that could have a better life outcome.

'If the court finds a violation of the convention or the protocols... and the internal law of the high contracting party concerned allows only partial reparation to be made, the court shall, if necessary, afford just satisfaction to the injured party'.[501]

There is compensation for pecuniary damage, non –pecuniary damage, costs and expenses. Placing the applicant in the position they were in, but for the violation, *'restitution in integrum'*. That is, actual loss (*'damnum emergens'*), 'diminished gain', future loss (*'lucrum cessans')[502]*.

Other potential legal remedies include *negligence, deceit or actionable misstatement.* Proceedings can be initiated at the appropriate court or tribunal.

Further potential relief

Government guidance indicates,[503] further relief by statutory prescription under s.234 (4) 1981 before expiry of six weeks after vesting.[504]

Additionally, *'estoppel or legitimate expectation'*, is a potential consideration for CPO affected applicants. As Lord Hoffman observed, *while, 'the right to a home has a high degree of protection, ordinary property rights are in general far more limited by considerations of public interest'.[505]* Hence, *without demonstration of that 'public interest' estoppel could be argued by the claimants.*

---

[500] article-41, https://www.coe.int

[501] article-41, https://www.coe.int

[502] article-41, https://www.coe.int

[503] https://www.gov.uk/government/publications/compulsory-purchase-process-and-the-crichel-down-rules-guidance

[504] J.P.L 2010,5 552-556

[505] Alec Samuels, The planning process and judicial control: the case for better judicial involvement and control,J.P.L 1570

However, the Supreme Court has ruled that whilst local Authorities have the powers to revoke planning permission, they must take into account cost considerations[506]. For affected residents, the balance should be weighed towards human rights of settled communities whose lives have been affected.

States can also issue measures like payment, reopening of proceedings, changes to legislation and discontinuation of proceedings.[507]

But neither Art 13 nor the convention in general, appear to require contradicting states to implement provisions of convention in any particular manner.

Damages under HRA are subject to a limitation period in tandem with Art 6 and are not recoverable as of right. But in accordance with the principle of 'just satisfaction' for the injured party, considered to be only in exceptional circumstances.[508]

Hence a need for greater states emphasis on human rights in CPOs to mitigate the detrimental impact against longstanding communities,[509] but could require regulatory reform.

International law [510]

A1P1 refers to principles of international law.[511]

Interestingly, in Lithgow v UK and James v UK, reference to 'principles[512] of international law[513]' was limited to non-nationals'.

---

[506] The Health and Safety Executive (Appellant) v Wolverhampton City Council (Respondent) [2012] UKSC 34 *On appeal from [2010] EWCA Civ 892*

[507] Mowbray, A. (2002). Duties of Investigation under the European Convention on Human Rights. *International and Comparative Law Quarterly, 51*(2), 437-448. doi:10.1093/iclq/51.2.437

[508] JUST SPACE / JUST SPACE ECONOMY AND PLANNING GROUP A response to the Mayor's document A City for All Londoners 11 December 2016

[509] *SEE planning commission suggestion insert in reforms Alec Samuels, The planning process and judicial control: the case for better judicial involvement and control,J.P.L 2007, 1570-1577*

[510] https://www.ohchr.org

[511] Egon Scweb, The Protection of the Right of Property of Nationals under the First Protocol to the European Convention on Human Rights, *The American Journal of Comparative Law* Vol. 13, No. 4 (Autumn, 1964), pp. 518-541

[512] Deborah Rook, Property Law and Human rights, 2001

[513] https://www.ohchr.org/en/professionalinterest/pages/internationallaw.aspx

It would appear that the architects of ECHR's strategic intentions were to allow non-nationals to secure their convention rights, directly, without the inbuilt disadvantages they face in the national legal system.

There is, however, international scrutiny as evidenced by a report from UNRA rapporteur on human rights.[514]

Professor Philip Alston observes that a wealthy country with the 'fifth' largest economy in the world should not be 'patently unjust and contrary to British values that so many people are living in poverty'[515]. Quoting the Institute for Fiscal Studies which foresees, 'a 7% rise in child poverty between 2015 and 2022, and various sources predict child poverty rates of as high as 40%'.

The report further notes that 'almost one in every two children to be poor in twenty-first century Britain is not just a disgrace, but a social calamity and an economic disaster, all rolled into one'.

Emphasising that, 'many of the recent changes to social support in the UK have a disparate impact on children'. Citing evidence from the Equality and Human Rights Commission which predicts that 'another 1.5 million more children will fall into poverty between 2010 and 2021/22 as a result of the changes to benefits and taxes, a 10% increase from 31% to 41%.'

According to Professor Philip Alston, the Social Metrics Commission, states that *'almost a third of children in the UK live in poverty. After years of progress, child poverty is rising again, and expected to continue increasing sharply in the coming years.'*

The report points to the legal aid cuts, 'in England and Wales since 2012 overwhelmingly affected the poor and people with disabilities, many of whom cannot otherwise afford to challenge benefit denials or reductions and are thus effectively deprived of their human right to a remedy', singling out ' the LASPO Act (Legal Aid, Sentencing and Punishment of Offenders Act) gutted the scope of cases that are handled, ratcheted up the level of means-tested eligibility criteria, and substituted telephonic for many previously face-to-face advice services'.

---

[514]Statement on visit to the United Kingdom, by Professor Philip Alston, United Nations Special Rapporteur on extreme poverty and human rights, https://www.ohchr.org/Documents/Issues/Poverty/EOM_GB_16Nov2018.pdf
[515] **Professor Philip Alston, United Nations Special Rapporteur on extreme poverty and human rights**

Prof. Alston concludes that *'It was a British philosopher, Thomas Hobbes, who memorably claimed that without a social contract; life outside society would be "solitary, poor, nasty, brutish, and short.*

The risk is that if current policies do not change, this is the direction in which low-income earners and the poor are headed. Loneliness, life expectancy rates have stalled in the United Kingdom' while 'at the same time many of the public places and institutions that previously brought communities together, such as libraries, community and recreation centres and public parks, have been steadily dismantled or undermined'.[516]

Professor Philip Alston's report is relevant for CPO affected residents. Such as a lack of access to legal aid, a disproportionate impact on children, racial minorities, the disabled, elderly and other socially historically disadvantaged communities.

This is potentially inconsistent with international conventions and international law. Specifically the Universal Declaration of Human Rights[517], which highlights ICCPR (1st generation rights)[518], ICESCR (second generation rights)[519], CERD /ICE (in relation to racial discrimination)[520] and CROC (convention on the right of children 1989.[521]

The report cited above, refers to the legal aid 'cuts' 'in England and Wales since 2012 which overwhelmingly affected the poor or people with disabilities. *Professor Philip Alston's report* is relevant for CPO affected residents. Such as lack of access to legal aid, a disproportionate impact on children, racial minorities, the disabled, elderly and historically disadvantaged communities.

This appears inconsistent with international conventions and international law. Such as the Universal Declaration of Human Rights[522], ICCPR (1st generation rights)[523], ICESCR (second generation rights)[524], CERD /ICE (in relation to racial discrimination)[525] and CROC (convention on the right of children 1989.[526]

---

[516] Report from UNRA rapporteur on human rights, **by Professor Philip Alston, United Nations Special Rapporteur on extreme poverty and human rights**
https://www.ohchr.org/Documents/Issues/Poverty/EOM_GB_16Nov2018.pdf
[517] Universal Declaration of Human rights, http://www.un.org/en/universal-declaration-human-rights/
[518] International convention on civil and political rights,
https://www.ohchr.org/EN/ProfessionalInterest/Pages/CCPR.aspx
[519] International convention on social and economic
rights,https://www.ohchr.org/en/professionalinterest/pages/cescr.aspx
[520] Committee on elimination of racial discrimination,
https://www.ohchr.org/en/hrbodies/cerd/pages/cerdindex.aspx
[521] Convention on the right of a Child,
https://www.ohchr.org/EN/ProfessionalInterest/Pages/CRC.aspx
[522] Universal Declaration of Human rights, http://www.un.org/en/universal-declaration-human-rights/

These conventions aim to protect economic, social, political rights of individuals or groups, such a rights relating to protection for the home, family, health, racial minorities, access to justice and due process. Although enforceability and applicability and legal jurisdiction over member states remains a potent legal hurdle.

The Universal Declaration Human rights, specifically refers to 'common understanding' of a set of values applicable to the treatment of individual human beings, irrespective of their race, religion, gender or other protected characteristics.[527]

But it is difficult to envisage this as a practical immediate relief to residents affected by CPOs. It would require measures to be implemented by the faulting nation states through protracted legal and political mechanisms.

Chapter 14

Proposals for reform

There are more recommendations by resident groups some of which are mirrored above.[528]

But in brief the central themes are improvement in consultation, transparency, scrutiny of financial viability or funding claims, rigorous assessment of social or affordable housing, protection of residents health/safety, compensation that

---

[523]International convention on civil and political rights, https://www.ohchr.org/EN/ProfessionalInterest/Pages/CCPR.aspx

[524] International convention on social and economic rights,https://www.ohchr.org/en/professionalinterest/pages/cescr.aspx

[525] Committee on elimination of racial discrimination, https://www.ohchr.org/en/hrbodies/cerd

[526] Convention on the right of a Child, https://www.ohchr.org

[527] https://www.un.org/en/universal-declaration-human-rights/

[528] https://savecressingham.wordpress.com/2017/03/14/cressinghams-recommendations-to-the-mayor-of-london

prevents dislocation from settled localities, access to legal advice/adjudication, rehousing and fair expeditious, independent process.

Arguably, the central or lingering causation of most of the difficulties associated with CPOs is the fusion of acquiring authorities with planning authorities and their close ties with the developers.

The law commission suggested proposals[529] for reform.[530] There have been modest amendments to existing legislation.[531]Recommendations should[532] aim at preventing dispossession, dislocation, disenfranchisement and detrimental financial impact on residents.

Through equitable compensation, meaningful consultation,[533] ensuring 'affordable housing,[534] racial equality[535], environmental protection[536]and safeguarding existing communities.[537]There are compelling proposals from residents,[538] campaigners[539]and government.[540]
For brevity and ease of reference these are set out in the format below.

- Community land trusts.[541].
- Codified legal protection of residents.[542]
- Separate Acquiring Authorities from planning.
- Independent planning body.
- Set CPO time limits.
- Human rights protection enforcement.

---

[529] Towards-a-compulsory-purchase-code, https://www.lawcom.gov.uk/

[530] Towards-a-compulsory-purchase-code, https://www.lawcom.gov.uk/

[531] SEE LCA 1961, 65 AND 73, The Localism Act 2011, Part 9 and the Neighbourhood Planning Act 2017, Part 2

[532] *DCLG, Estate Regeneration National Strategy Resident Engagement and Protection; draft-good-practice-guide-to-estate-regeneration-main-consultation-summary-report.pdf*
https://www.london.gov.uk,

[533] staying-put-an-anti-gentrification-handbook-for-council-estates-in-london/
https://justspace.org.uk

[534] JUST SPACE / JUST SPACE ECONOMY AND PLANNING GROUP, A response to the Mayor's document A City for All Londoners 11 December 2016

[535] Jessica Perera, The London Clearances, Race, Housing and Policing,

[536] JUST SPACE / JUST SPACE ECONOMY AND PLANNING GROUP A response to the Mayor's document A City for All Londoners 11 December 2016

[537] Equalities **https://justspacelondon.files.wordpress.com/2018/12/m2-js-equalities.pdf**

[538]https://grenfellactiongroup.wordpress.com; http://www.defendcouncilhousing.org.uk/dch/; http://radicalhousingnetwork.org/; https://grenfellactiongroup.wordpress.com; saveWestburysw8; https://architectsforsocialhousing.wordpress.com; Westbury-a-year-after-Grenfell/ http://housingactivists.co.uk
/Grenfell/Westbury-a-year-after-Grenfell

[539] https://justspace.org.uk

[540]Estate regeneration good practice guide, https://www.gov.uk

[541] Brett Christophers, The New Enclosures, the Appropriation of Public Land in Neoliberal Britain

[542]Stuart Hodkinson (2011) The Private Finance Initiative in English Council Housing Regeneration: A Privatisation too Far?, Housing Studies, 26:6, 911-932, DOI: 10.1080/02673037.2011.593133
; mill wall-the-den-cpo-scheme-Lewisham-council
https://www.theguardian.com/football/2017/jan/24

- Rigorous environmental enforcement.
- Timely and mandatory disclosure of CPO related contracts.
- Statutory access to legal assistance.
- PSED[543] independent assessment.
- Preference for refurbishment.[544]
- Independent body examining life outcomes of CPOs[545].
- Quantifiable statutory damages.
- Right to balloting of residents should be a legal requirement.
- Expeditious enforcement of the rehousing duty under s39 of 1973.
- Families with young children to expediently be prioritised.[546]
- Leasehold reform.
- Like for like exchange for leaseholders.
- CPO shared[547] ownerships schemes[548] review.
- Shared equity requirement.
- Legal prohibition of councillors working for developers immediately after or during their public service.
- FCA should be part and parcel of financial scrutiny.
- Emphasis of local economic direct benefit should be a legal requirement.
- Financial Auditors to be independent of acquiring authorities.
- Consultations should be community driven.

Conclusion

This text has explored the legal requirements, justification, implementation process, adverse impact on communities and the consequential incompatibility of CPOs with human rights[549].

As indicated above, there has been privatisation of public land over the long-term; in which CPOs is just part of the weapons in the tool box creating inequality.[550]Consequently raising questions whether that has 'led to regeneration which has made us more fearful of each other and intensified

---

[543] S149 EA2010

[544] our-work/re-thinking-housing/demolition-or-refurbishment-social-housing-london, https://www.ucl.ac.uk/grand-challenges/sustainable-cities/

[545] **Health Impact Assessment,** edited by John Kemm, Jayne Parry, Stephen Palmer, Stephen R. Palmer

[546] Children and their Urban Environment: Changing Worlds, by Claire Freeman, Paul Tranter

[547] Paul Watt (2009) Housing Stock Transfers, Regeneration and State-Led Gentrification in London, Urban Policy and Research, 27:3, 229-242, DOI: 10.1080/08111140903154147

[548]Richardson V Midland Heart; https://www.theguardian.com/housing-network/hidden-dangers-shared-ownership

[549] Phil Hubbard & Loretta Lees (2018) The right to community?, City, 22:1, 8-25, DOI: 10.1080/13604813.2018.1432178

[550] Brett Christophers,The New Enclosures, the Appropriation of Public Land in Neoliberal Brit

social divisions'.[551] Where CPOs are tools in 'neo –liberal Britain'[552] that legitimise documented 'hostile' land acquisition.[553].

The choices appear onerous for residents.

Choosing between demolition of homes without active involvement or acquiesce to gross interference in their lives, family and home environment.[554] The emerging theme appears to confirm the real prospect of CPO incompatibility with human rights.[555]

Manifested through unfair processes and adverse outcomes. Thereby accentuating a need for urgent reform to protect long-term settled communities[556] or small businesses.[557]

Even worse the adverse impact appears to be disproportionate to racial minorities.[558] Which further highlight the need for human rights protections to be a central focus before, during and after the CPO process.[559]

A failure to implement human rights protections risks regarding the ECHR,[560] HRA[561] or international instruments[562]as academic or harmless beasts or as Douglas Maxwell ponders, poses the question, whether A1P1 'a paper tiger'?[563]

To extinguish such legitimate descriptions, there is an urgent need for human rights[564] to be at the centre of CPOs processes, decisions and outcomes. To

---

[551] Anna Minton, Ground Control, Fear and Happiness in the twenty first century City

[552] Brett Christophers,The New Enclosures, the Appropriation of Public Land in Neoliberal Brit

[553] Jessica Perera, London clearances, Race, Housing and policing,http://www.irr.org.uk

[554] Phil Hubbard & Loretta Lees (2018) The right to community?, City, 22:1, 8-25, DOI: 10.1080/13604813.2018.1432178

[555] Sarah Nield (2013) Article 8 Respect for the Home: A Human Property Right?, King's Law Journal, 24:2, 147-171, DOI: 10.5235/09615768.24.2.147

[556]Alice Balotti, Estate Regeneration and Community Impacts Challenges and lessons for social landlords, developers and local councils, 2016, http://sticerd.lse.ac.uk/dps/case/cr/casereport99.pdf

[557] Traders-win-court-of-appeal-battle-over-shepherd-s-bush-market-regeneration https://www.publiclawtoday.co.uk/planning/438-planning-features-

[558] ethnic-inequalities-London-capital-all https://www.trustforlondon.org.uk

[559]Javid-rejects-Aylesbury-estate-cpo-as-breach-of-human-rights,

https://www.architectsjournal.co.uk

[560] Kenna, P. (2008). Housing rights: positive duties and enforceable rights at the European Court of Human Rights. European Human Rights Law Review, 13(2), 193-208

[561] Kenna, P. (2008). Housing rights: positive duties and enforceable rights at the European Court of Human Rights. European Human Rights Law Review, 13(2), 193-208

[562] https://www.ohchr.org/en/professionalinterest/pages/cescr.aspx

[563] Douglas Maxwell, Journal of planning & Environmental Law, Article 1 of the First protocol: A paper tiger in the face of compulsory purchase orders for private profit?

[564] Adélaïde Remiche, *Yordanova and Others v Bulgaria*: The Influence of the Social Right to Adequate Housing on the Interpretation of the Civil Right to Respect for One's Home, *Human Rights Law Review*, Volume 12, Issue 4, December 2012, Pages 787–800, https://doi.org/10.1093/hrlr/ngs033

avoid total abdication of human rights to the whims and primal instincts of profit focused developers or entities, with potentially complicit acquiring authorities.[565]

This would avoid what Anna Minton describes, *'as control and segregation of every aspect of city life, an American model…Instead of …a healthier approach to public life, culture and democracy that would reinvigorate civic engagement in Britain'.*

The alternative is a free for all, winner takes it all approach which leaves communities' health potentially at the mercy of the complicity, inaction and collaboration of opaque financial practices[566] and unaccountable planning authorities.[567]Shaking the very fabric of a fair democratic, progressive society in which one's property and inherent intrinsic corresponding rights should be protected de jure and de facto. A human rights system that can be meaningfully enforced and retains the confidence of wider society. Since societies are reportedly judged by how they treat the weakest in society,[568] there is an obvious need for human rights protection to be a fundamental tenet of any society.

After all human rights should be universal[569] as well as erga omnes.[570]

As succinctly put by Art 1 and 2 of UDHR, which respectively state that; *All human beings are born free and equal in dignity and rights. They are endowed with reason and conscience and should act towards one another in a spirit of brotherhood;*

Everyone is entitled to all the rights and freedoms set forth in this Declaration, without distinction of any kind, such as race, colour, sex, language, religion, political or other opinion, national or social origin, property, birth or other status. Furthermore, no distinction shall be made on the basis of the political, jurisdictional or international status of the country or territory to which a

---

[565] Peter Newman ' Ian Smith' Cultural production, place and politics on the South Bank of the Thames, First published: 28 June 2008

[566] Jerry Flynn (2016) Complete control, City, 20:2, 278-286, DOI: 10.1080/13604813.2016.1143685

[567] London-council-aylesbury-estate-development-southwark-financial-risk,

https://www.theguardian.com,

[568] Attributed to Ghandi et al

[569] https://www.un.org/en/universal-declaration-human-rights/

[570] Kadelbach, S. (2006). "Chapter II. Jus Cogens, Obligations Erga Omnes and Other Rules - the Identification of Fundamental Norms". In The Fundamental Rules of the International Legal Order. Boston, USA: Brill | Nijhoff. doi: https://doi.org/10.1163/ej.9789004149816.i-472.10

person belongs, whether it be independent, trust, non-self-governing or under any other limitation of sovereignty'.[571]

It remains to be seen how that basic human rights 'universality' will be manifested in CPO implementation.

Bibliography

1.   MHCLG: Guidance on compulsory purchase process and the Crichel down Rules for the disposal of surplus land acquired by, or under the threat of, compulsion, https://www.gov.uk/government/publications/compulsory-purchase-process-and-the-crichel-down-rules-guidance.
2.   The Implications of Kilo in Land Use Law, Symposium Articles: Keynote Address - Kelo, Lingle, and San Remo Hotel, Santa Clara Law Review, Vol. 46, Issue 4 (2006), pp. 787-810 Curtin, Daniel J. Jr
3.   Globalization, Communities and Human Rights: Community-Based Property Rights and Prior Informed Consent,2006 Sutton Colloquium Article, Denver Journal of International Law and Policy, Vol. 35, Issue 3 & 4 (Summer-Fall 2007),pp. 413 428 https://heinonline.org/419

---

[571] https://www.un.org/en/universal-declaration-human-rights/index.html

4.   Human Rights and Property Rights [article] United States Law Review, Vol. 64, Issue 11 (November 1930), pp. 581-594 Blume, Fred H.

5.   Equating Human Rights and Property Rights--The Need for Moral Judgement in an Economic Analysis of Law and Social Policy, Ohio State Law Journal, Vol. 47, Issue 1 (1986), pp. 163-200 Malloy, Robin Paul

6.   Douglas Maxwell, Journal of planning & Environmental Law, Article 1 of the First protocol: A paper tiger in the face of compulsory purchase orders for private profit?

7.   Towards a Compulsory Purchase Code: https://www.lawcom.gov.uk/project/towards-a-compulsory-purchase-code/

8.   Compulsory acquisition of land: Developers, by PLC Property https://uk.practicallaw.thomsonreuters.com

9.   Planning Act 2016: http://www.housing.org.uk/resource-library/browse/the-housing-and- planning-act-2016/

10.   Kept in the Dark; https://www.transparency.org.uk

11.   The Law of compulsory purchase, third edition, Guy Roots et al

12.   Estate-regeneration-why-people-power-is-forcing-london-to-rethink-housing; developers-alarmed-at-khans-plans-to-give-estate-residents-power; https://www.architectsjournal.co.uk/news

13.   Mayor-and-conservatives-dispute-latest-London-housing-stats; https://www.insidehousing.co.uk/news/news/ https://www.bbc.co.uk

14.   Phil Hubbard, Loretta Lees. (2018) the right to community? *City* 22:1, pages 8-25.

15.   https://www.transparency.org.uk/faulty-towers

16.   https://architectsforsocialhousing.wordpress.com/2016/03/24/the-doomsday-book/).

17.   Towards a paradigm of Southern urbanism Seth Schindler City Volume 21, 2017 - Issue 1Published online: 6 Mar 2017

18.   Reconstructing Berlin: Materiality and meaning in the symbolic politics of urban space

19.   Dominik Bartmanski et al.City Volume 22, 2018 - Issue 2 Published online: 17 Apr 2018

20.   Editorial Editor-in-Chief's note: What/whose order is to be asserted in the city?

21.   Bob Catterall City Volume 22, 2018 - Issue 2

22.   Published online: 7 Jun 2018

23.   The right to community?: Legal geographies of resistance on London's gentrification frontiers

24.   Phil Hubbard et al. City Volume 22, 2018 - Issue 1 Published online: 15 Mar 2018 editorial

25.   Editorial: The right to assert the order of things in the city Luke R. Barnesmoore City

26.   Volume 22, 2018 - Issue 2 Published online: 7 Jun 2018

27.   Stuart Hodkinson, Chris Essen, (2015) "Grounding accumulation by dispossession in everyday life: The unjust geographies of urban regeneration under the Private Finance Initiative", International Journal of Law in the Built Environment, Vol. 7 Issue: 1, pp.72-91, https://doi.org/10.1108/IJLBE-01-2014-0007

28.   Towards a new perspective on the role of the city in social movements: Urban Policy after the 'Arab Spring' Raffael Beier City Volume 22, 2018 - Issue 2 Published online: 17 Apr 2018

29.   Adonis, A., and B. Davies, eds. 2015. City Villages: More Homes, Better Communities. London: IPPR. https://www.ippr.org/publications/city-villages-more-homes-better-communities

30.   The London Borough of Southwark (Aylesbury Estate Site 1B-1C) Compulsory Purchase Order 2014 ('the Order': http://35percent.org/img/Decision_Letter_Final.pdf

31. Prime minister pledges to transform sink estates: https://www.gov.uk/government/news/prime-minister-pledges-to-transform-sink-estates: 10 January 2016

32. 'Cameron time to demolish sink estates': https://www.bbc.co.uk/news/av/uk-politics-35275516/cameron-time-to-demolish-worst-sink-housing-estates, 10 January 2016

33. Compulsory purchase and Compensation: An Overview of the system in England and Wales, By Frances Plimmer.

34. Paul Watt & Anna Minton (2016) London's housing crisis and its activisms, City, 20:2, 204-221, https://doi.org/10.1080/13604813.2016.1151707

35. Participation in the right of access to adequate housing, 14 Tulsa J Comp. & Intl L 269 2006 -2007, Hein online

36. Republic of SA v Grootboom & others 2000(11) BCLR 1169

37. Evadne Grant, Enforcing Social and Economic Rights: The right to adequate housing in south Africa, 15 Afr, J, intl & Comp,L 1 (2007), Hein online

38. The requirements for a compelling case in the public interest to justify a CPO (High Court) by Practical Law Planning: In Horada v Secretary of State for Communities and Local Government [2015] EWHC 2512 (Admin), Volume: 25 issue: 1, page(s): 115-135

39. The privatization of council housing, Norman Ginsburg, Issue published: February 1, 2005 https://doi.org/10.1177%2F0261018305048970

40. Haringey Council votes to cancel development vehicle despite Lendlease warning 18 July   2018:https://www.insidehousing.co.uk/news/news/haringey-council-votes-to-cancel-development-vehicle-despite-lendlease-warning-57250:

41. Watt, P. 2015. "The IMD as a WMD in the Regeneration of London Council Estates: Tackling Spatial Inequalities and Producing Socio-spatial Injustice." Paper at Tackling Spatial Inequalities Conference, Sheffield, September 10

42. Paul Watt (2009) Housing Stock Transfers, Regeneration and State-Led Gentrification in London, Urban Policy and Research, 27:3, 229-242, https://doi.org/10.1080/08111140903154147

43. Pam Douglas & Joanne Parkes (2016) 'Regeneration' and 'consultation' at a Lambeth council estate, City, 20:2, 287-291, https://doi.org/10.1080/13604813.2016.1143683

44. Bracking V Secretary of state for works and pensions [2013] EWCA Civ 1345, [2014] Eq LR 60

45. Knock it down or Do it UP? The challenge of estate regeneration https://www.london.gov.uk/about-us/london-assembly/london-assembly-publications/knock-it-down-or-do-it

46. HPA 2016 and how it affects housing associations: http://www.lag.org.uk/magazine/2016/07/a-devastating-blow-to-social-housing-in-england.aspx

47. EA2010Equality Act 2010 (Specific Duties and Public Authorities) Regulations 2017. PSED: specific duties in England, Practical Law UK Practice Note

48. CPA 1965: Compulsory Purchase Act 1965.

49. CP (VD) A 1981: Compulsory Purchase (Vesting Declarations) Act 1981.

50. LCA 1961: Land Compensation Act 1961.

51. LCA 1973: Land Compensation Act 1973.

52. TCPA 1990: Town and Country Planning Act 1990

53. https://www.libertyhumanrights.org.uk/

54. https://www.equalityhumanrights.com/en/about-us

55. https://www.ohchr.org/en/professionalinterest/pages/ccpr.aspx

56. https://echr.coe.int/

57. British Institute of human rights www.Bihr.org.uk

58.   Chartered Institute of Housing www. Cih.org

59.   DCLG www.coommunites.gov.uk

60.   Housing Law practitioners Association www. Hipa.org.uk

61.   The Law Society www.lawsociety.org

62.   https://savecressingham.wordpress.com/

63.   http://www.insidehousing.co.uk/cressingham-gardens-regeneration-approved-in-high-court/7018185.article

64.   http://35percent.org/2013-06-08-the-heygate-diaspora/

65.   https://www.southwarknews.co.uk/news/council-given-permission-take-aylesbury-estate-cpo-case-high-court-disappointing-blow-campaigners/

66.   http://www.shelter.org.uk

67.   http://www.axethehousingact.org.uk/page/2/ on

68.   Localism Act 2011, https://uk.practicallaw.thomsonreuters.com/1-504-2706

69.   Housing and equality law, By Robert Brown, Arden Chambers

a.   https://uk.practicallaw.thomsonreuters.com/w-012-0034

70.   https://www.ashurst.com/en/news-and-insights/legal-updates/compulsory-purchase-life-after-aylesbury/

71.   https://www.birketts.co.uk/insights/legal-updates/compulsory-purchase-and-what-to-do-about-it

72.   https://assets.publishing.service.gov.uk/government/uploads/system/uploads/attachment_data/file/551698/ECHR_Memorandum.pdf

73.   https://www.burges-salmon.com/news-and-insight/legal-updates/alternative-development-proposals-how-do-they-affect-cpo-validity/

74.   Housing and Regeneration Act 2008, Housing and Regeneration Act 2008

a.   http://www.opsi.gov.uk/acts/acts2008/ukpga_20080017_en_1

75.   Donnelly, Jack. Universal human rights in theory and practice. Cornell University Press, 2013.

76.   Human rights Act 1998: https://uk.practicallaw.thomsonreuters.com/0-506-9287

77.   Lexis   Nexis: https://www.lexisnexis.com/uk/lexispsl/publiclaw/document/413481/5DF5-Dealing_with_a_human_rights_challengehttps://www.lexisnexis.com/uk/lexispsl/publicl

78.   New law journal: https://www.newlawjournal.co.uk/

79.   Practicallaw:https://uk.practicallaw.thomsonreuters.com/Browse/Home/Practice/PublicLaw

80.   Hansard- https://hansard.parliament.uk/

81.   https://www.leighday.co.uk/News/2015/November-2015/Cressingham-Gardens-tenant-wins-High-Court-legal

82.   https://www.theguardian.com/commentisfree/2017/oct/25/labour-council-regeneration-housing-crisis-high-court-judge

83.   The Secretary of states' ruling re: Town and Country Planning Act 1990 Section 226(1) (a), Acquisition of Land Act 1981 The London Borough of Southwark (Aylesbury Estate Site 1B-1C) Compulsory Purchase Order 2014 ('

84.   https://hsfnotes.com/realestatedevelopment/2016/09/28/a-new-right-to-a-community-decision-by-the-secretary-of-state-not-to-confirm-the-cpo-for-aylesbury-estate/

85.   Compulsory_purchase_process_and_the_Crichel_Down_Rules_-_guidance_updated_180228;https://assets.publishing.service.gov.uk/government/uploads/system/uploads/attachment_data/file/684529/

86.   http://www.legislation.gov.uk/ukpga/2010/15/

87.   https://www.burges-salmon.com/news-and-insight/legal-updates/the-neighbourhood-planning-act-2017/

88.   https://www.legislation.gov.uk/ukpga/2010/15/section/149

89.   https://assets.publishing.service.gov.uk/government/uploads/system/uploads/attachment_data/file/475271/cpo_guidance.pdf

90.   Knock It Down Or Do It Up; https://www.london.gov.uk/sites/default/files/gla_migrate_files_destination/

91.   London's Housing Crisis Worse for Ethnic Minorities 22 March 2016;;https://www.runnymedetrust.org/news/638/272

92.   Dispossession the great social housing swindle: https://www.dispossessionfilm.com/

93.   City Villages, More Homes, Better communities: https://www.ippr.org/files/publications/pdf/city-villages_Mar2015.pdf

94.   Shelter. 2015. Homes for our Children. How much of the Housing Market is Affordable?,https://england.shelter.org.uk/Homes_for_our_Children.pdf

95.   The-story-of-the-camberwell-submarine-4618, https://www.insidehousing.co.uk/insight/insight

96.   Convention for the Protection of Individuals with regard to Automatic Processing of Personal Data Strasbourg, 28.I.1981 https://rm.coe.int/CoE

97.   Legal Challenges to Implementing CPOs and Decisions under the Crichel down Rules by Tim Mould QC http://www.landmarkchambers.co.uk/userfiles/TM.pdf

98.   The use of compulsory purchase powers for regeneration by Elvin QC, http://www.landmarkchambers.co.uk s. 149 of the Equality Act 2010

99.   Land Compensation Claims: The Claimants Perspective by Simon Pickles Landmark Chambers   http://www.landmarkchambers.co.uk/cases-compulsory_purchase_compensation.aspx

100.   Compulsory purchase orders: stage 4, CPO compensation procedure: flowchart by Practical Law Planning, https://uk.practicallaw.thomsonreuters.com/2-629-7353

101.   Twenty years later-Assessing the significance of the Human Rights Act 1998 to the residential possession proceedings, By Ian Loveland http://openaccess.city.ac.uk/17163/

102.   Housing Act 1988 https://www.legislation.gov.uk/id/ukpga/1988/50

103.   R on the application of Sainsbury's supermarket ltd) V Wolverhampton city Council (2010) UKSC

104.   Waters v welsh development agency (2004)1WLR 1304

105.   David Elvin QC paper, Use of compulsory purchase powers for regeneration, http://www.landmarkchambers.co.uk

106.   Countryside Alliance v Attorney General [2007] UKHL 52

107.   Article 1 of the first Protocol to the ECHR: protection of property, Practical Law UK Practice Note, https://uk.practicallaw.thomsonreuters.com/8-385-5732

108.   Article 6 of the ECHR: right to a fair hearing Housing:

109.   https://uk.practicallaw.thomsonreuters.com/2-385-8106

110.   Part VII of the Housing Act 1996, https://uk.practicallaw.thomsonreuters.com

111.   Demolition or refurbishment of social housing? https://www.ucl.ac.uk/engineering-exchange/research-projects/2018/nov/demolition-or-refurbishment-social-housing

112.   Stanton, J. (2014). The Big Society and Community Development: Neighbourhood Planning under the Localism Act. Environmental Law Review, 16(4), 262–276.

113.   Murungaru v Home Secretary [2008] EWCA Civ 1015

114.   Fazia Ali v The United Kingdom - 40378/10 Court (Fourth Section)) [2015] ECHR 924

115. Belfast City Council v Miss Behavin' Ltd [2007] UKHL 19
116. James V UK (A98 (1986 E.H.R.R 123 (ECHR)
117. Sporrong and Lönnroth [1982] 5 EHRR 35
118. Le Compte, Van Leuven and De Meyere v Belgium [1981] ECHR 3.
119. Bryan v United Kingdom [1995] ECHR 50, (1996) 21 EHRR 342
120. Begum v London Borough of Tower Hamlets [2003] UKHL 5
121. Lithgow and others v UK [1986] 8 EHRR 329)
122. Chapman v. the United Kingdom [GC], § 96;
123. Yordanova and Others v. Bulgaria, §§ 129-130
124. Zehentner v. Austria, §§ 63 and 65) / (A.-M.V. v. Finland, §§ 82-84 and 90).
125. Qazi v Harrow LBC (2003 UKHL 43: (2004) 1 AC 983 (HL)
126. Salvesen V Riddell(2013) UKSC 22: 2013 SC(U.K.S.C) 236(SC)
127. López Ostra v. Spain, §§ 56-58,
128. Moreno Gómez v. Spain, § 61.
129. Di Sarno and Others v. Italy, § 112).
130. Hatton and Others v. the United Kingdom [GC], § 96;
131. Moreno Gómez v. Spain, § 53)
132. Fadeyeva v. Russia, § 69.
133. (Asselbourg and Others v. Luxembourg (dec.)).
134. Martínez Martínez and Pino Manzano v. Spain,
135. (Hardy and Maile v. the United Kingdom
136. (Hatton and Others v. the United Kingdom [GC]
137. https://www.facebook.com/Savewestburysw8-804075296314550/
138. https://twitter.com/savewestburysw8

1ˢᵗ edition MAY 2019